The Soul's Journey

Rebirth and the Justice of Karma

By

Jonathan W. Hale

Preface

to *The Soul's Journey: Rebirth and the Justice of Karma*
by **Jonathan W. Hale**

What if your life, as you now live it, is just one chapter in a much larger, eternal story? What if the trials you face, the talents you possess, and even the people you're drawn to are not random at all, but woven from a thread that stretches far beyond this moment, this body, this lifetime?

This book, *The Soul's Journey: Rebirth and the Justice of Karma*, was born from the growing awareness that the modern world—despite its advances—still aches for meaning. Beneath the noise of society, many of us are quietly asking: Why am I here? Why do I suffer? Why do others thrive? Is there justice in the grand scheme of things? And most importantly—does it all matter?

The ancient doctrines of **reincarnation** and **karma** offer answers to these very questions—answers that are not only spiritually nourishing but deeply rational. These are not just mystical ideas for quiet meditation rooms or sacred temples—they are practical principles for living with awareness, responsibility, and peace.

My goal has been not to preserve dogma, but to breathe new life into eternal truths—truths that belong to no single culture or time period, but to the very nature of the soul itself.

A Universe That Remembers

One of the most profound realizations a human being can have is this: **The universe forgets nothing.**

Every action you take, every word you speak, every emotion you allow to move through you—these are not cast away into oblivion. They ripple outward. They leave impressions. They shape not only the world around you, but the invisible architecture of your inner being. And in the doctrine of karma, this invisible architecture follows you—not in judgment, but in precision.

Karma is often misunderstood in the West. Some equate it with punishment. Others view it as supernatural justice doled out by an unseen force. But karma, at its essence, is far more graceful and exact. It is simply **the law of cause and effect as it applies to consciousness**. Just as gravity governs the body, karma governs the soul. It is the feedback system of our moral and spiritual evolution. It doesn't judge—it mirrors. It doesn't punish—it teaches.

Karma is not fate. It is not destiny carved in stone. It is more like momentum, inviting you either to repeat old cycles or to break free through awareness. And through this law, we come to realize that **every moment matters**—not because we are being watched, but because we are being shaped.

Rebirth: Not a Belief, but a Pattern

Reincarnation, too, has been widely misunderstood. Often dismissed as religious folklore or romantic fantasy, it is, in truth, one of the most ancient and enduring explanations for the inequality and mystery of life. Why are we born into such different circumstances? Why does one child suffer and another sing? Why do some people seem wise beyond their years, while others never awaken?

The idea of rebirth offers not blind consolation, but **cosmic coherence**. It tells us that our soul's journey is not confined to the brief span between birth and death. It continues, moving forward from lifetime to lifetime, learning through contrast and growth. Each life is a classroom. Each relationship, a lesson. Each desire, a compass.

Reincarnation gives shape to the mystery of our longings, talents, and even our wounds. It assures us that **nothing is wasted**, and no life—however painful or brief—is without purpose. The soul carries forward what the mind forgets. And this continuity of learning across lifetimes is one of the most elegant illustrations of justice the universe can offer.

Beyond Reward and Punishment

One of the key shifts this book invites you to make is this: to stop seeing life through the lens of reward and punishment, and to begin seeing it through the lens of **growth**.

When we are young—spiritually and emotionally—we need rules, structure, and the promise of reward. We fear punishment. We seek approval. But as we mature, the deeper truth becomes evident: The universe is not punishing us—it is **responding** to us. It is shaping us through our own actions, patterns, choices, and intentions. It is offering correction, not condemnation.

You will find in the chapters ahead many interpretations of karma—some ancient and rigid, others modern and expansive. My intent is not to push one version upon you, but to offer a panorama of possibilities. Let your intuition guide you. Let your experience confirm what resonates. And above all, let go of the notion that karma is something to fear.

In fact, the only thing to fear is ignorance of how karma works. Once you begin to see it not as divine punishment, but as **spiritual education**, a great burden lifts. Suffering becomes a message, not a sentence. Mistakes become opportunities. And progress becomes possible—one conscious choice at a time.

A Philosophy for Modern Living

The Soul's Journey is not a book of religious instruction. It is a book of spiritual clarity. It is meant for the thoughtful skeptic as much as for the devoted seeker. You do not need to subscribe to any specific tradition to benefit from the ideas here. What you need, instead, is curiosity—a willingness to look within and a desire to see your life as part of something larger.

In our modern era of disconnection, distraction, and anxiety, we crave frameworks that explain why things happen and how we can live with purpose. Reincarnation and karma offer such a framework. They give us a long view, a cosmic patience, a faith that life is not random and that we are not powerless.

When viewed through this lens, you are not a victim of fate, nor a slave to circumstance. You are an active participant in your own unfolding. Even when life feels unjust, karma whispers, "Keep going—there is more to this story than you know."

The Soul's Justice

Justice in this universe is not found in courtrooms or human systems—it is embedded in the architecture of existence itself. The law of karma is not man-made—it is soul-made. And it is flawless in its design.

Does this mean every tragedy is deserved? Every misfortune karmic? No. Such oversimplifications are not only spiritually immature—they are often cruel. This book does not endorse that kind of shallow thinking. It acknowledges instead the **multi-dimensional complexity** of life, in which karma, free will, spiritual agreements, and collective evolution all intersect in mysterious ways.

Karma is never about blame—it is about **understanding**. And through understanding, we heal.

How to Read This Book

The chapters ahead have been written and reimagined with care. Each section offers a slightly different angle on the same eternal truth: That we are evolving souls in a just and conscious universe. Some chapters may feel philosophical; others more practical. Read them slowly. Pause when something resonates. Return when something puzzles you.

This is not a book to rush through—it is a book to grow with.

Let each idea land where it may. There is no final dogma here, no demand for belief. There is only invitation—to remember what you may have known once before… and to live as though it matters again.

Your Journey Is Already Underway

This is not the beginning for you.

You have walked this Earth before. You have loved, lost, stumbled, and risen many times. The soul you are today has been shaped by countless days and nights, joys and regrets, lessons and longings.

And you will walk again.

But this time—this life—you may walk differently. With more awareness. With more trust in the unseen guidance at work. With a deeper sense of responsibility for your thoughts, your actions, your relationships, and your growth.

If this book does anything, I hope it reminds you of the **dignity** of your soul's path. You are not lost. You are not broken. You are not late.

You are precisely where you need to be, learning precisely what your soul is ready to learn.

May these pages offer you light on that path. And may you always walk forward, not in fear—but in the quiet confidence that **all is well**, and that the soul's journey always bends toward truth, toward wholeness, and toward home.

With humility and hope,
Jonathan W. Hale

Chapter I: The Origins of Rebirth Beliefs

When we speak of *reincarnation*, we refer to the ongoing process by which the soul—the unseen, immaterial essence of a person—returns to physical existence again and again through new births. This concept, although ancient, has taken many names and forms across different cultures and times.

Some have used the word *metempsychosis* to describe a similar process—the migration of the soul, viewed as a timeless spiritual force, from one body into another after the physical form has died. Another term, *transmigration of souls*, is occasionally used as well, although it has often been tied to a different, more primitive version of the concept: the belief that a human soul could inhabit the body of an animal as a form of punishment. This latter view is generally seen as separate and even contradictory to the philosophies behind reincarnation and metempsychosis, which emphasize spiritual growth rather than retribution through degradation.

Although the idea of reincarnation has appeared in many forms, with varying levels of complexity and interpretation, there exists a central truth at the core of all these beliefs: the soul—also called the spirit, the higher self, or the inner being—is something beyond the reach of death. It lives on even after the body decays. After a certain period of rest or transition, this soul begins a new chapter by being born into a new physical form, often as an infant unaware of its spiritual past. And yet, the essence of its former experiences is not lost—it becomes part of the soul's evolving personality, shaping who it is and what it becomes in the new life.

It is widely believed among spiritual thinkers that this process of rebirth is not random. Rather, it follows a precise and just law—often called the law of attraction or karma—that ensures the soul returns to conditions that reflect its past choices, thoughts, and actions. In this way, the parents, the environment, and the circumstances into which one is born are not accidental, but rather intricately linked to the soul's journey. Each soul is drawn, by invisible justice, to the path it has prepared for itself.

E.D. Walker, a respected English scholar in this field, once described the idea in poetic and profound terms. He explained that reincarnation teaches us that when a soul is born into this world, it does not arrive as a blank slate or as some random gathering of matter that will dissolve into nothingness at death. Instead, each soul carries with it the hidden writings of many past lives—some familiar, others alien and ancient, spanning the distant reaches of time. These past lives leave impressions, invisible to the eye, but deeply embedded within the structure of the new life. Just like photographic images that remain unseen until developed, these karmic imprints shape our instincts, tendencies, and traits.

Every experience we live in the present is recorded in the subtle memory of the soul, even if we do not consciously recall it. These silent records influence our future lives, molding our character, guiding our preferences, and coloring our reactions. Our current physical traits, mental habits, emotional strengths, and even our weaknesses are the outcome of how we used the chances life once gave us. We are, in a very real sense, the inheritors of ourselves. Our fate is the harvest of seeds planted in forgotten fields of long-past lives.

In this vision of existence, there is no divine favoritism, no arbitrary gifts or punishments from an unseen force. Every soul is offered the same spiritual soil in which to grow. A man who now holds power and wealth may one day be humbled by poverty, just as the poor and diligent may rise in future lives to positions of influence and peace. Only the inner qualities of the soul travel with us from one existence to the next—the rest, including status and possessions, fade away. The lazy rich man of today may become the struggling wanderer of tomorrow, while the hardworking and kind-hearted woman may sow the seeds of future wisdom, strength, and joy.

In this view, suffering patiently endured becomes the root of resilience and courage in the next life. Obstacles transform into spiritual muscles. Acts of self-restraint and discipline refine the will. Tastes and talents nurtured in one lifetime blossom again later, and energies we have once cultivated continue their journey across the ages, returning whenever the conditions are right for them to manifest. Conversely, unconscious patterns, compulsions, and emotional habits—both noble and destructive—are the echoes of distant lives, following us like shadows until we transform them through awareness.

The belief in reincarnation—whether we call it metempsychosis, rebirth, or soul evolution—has been deeply rooted in the consciousness of humanity since time immemorial. Like a river that may disappear beneath the surface only to reemerge stronger downstream, this ancient teaching has endured through the rise and fall of civilizations. In some parts of the world, its flame has never flickered. In others, where it seemed to vanish, it has quietly reawakened, reigniting the interest of new generations of seekers.

The renewed interest in reincarnation in today's Western world is no accident—it follows the same cyclical rhythm that guides nature and thought alike. Ideas move in pendulum-like cycles: what once was accepted, then forgotten, returns again in new form. Many spiritual observers believe that we are on the threshold of a new age of understanding, in which the Western mind will once more embrace this ancient truth. What was once considered heretical or obsolete may soon become a guiding spiritual framework for the modern world. And yet, even if this renewed enthusiasm fades again with time, the doctrine will survive, as it always has, ready to return when minds and hearts are once more prepared to receive it.

It is important to note that reincarnation has never truly vanished from human thought. At every stage in history, some part of the human race has preserved it, and often, it has been the belief of the majority. Thousands of years ago, the ancient peoples of India and the Far East held it sacred—and so they do to this very day. The millions of Hindus, Buddhists, and other spiritual groups across Asia continue to uphold reincarnation as a foundational truth of existence. Even outside these traditions, scattered through both Eastern and Western cultures, we find traces of the idea—sometimes hidden in myth, sometimes surviving in ritual or superstition, but always there, breathing just beneath the surface of belief.

When we trace the origins of this doctrine through ancient civilizations, we find no clear point of invention. No single culture can be credited with having "created" the concept. Whether it flourished in ancient Egypt, India, or in the lost lands of forgotten continents like Atlantis, the idea itself seems to have emerged wherever human consciousness grew deep enough to question life, death, and what lies beyond. Reincarnation appears not as a manufactured theory, but as a natural conclusion drawn by minds beginning to awaken to the mysteries of the soul's journey.

Even the most primitive of societies, when they developed a notion of a soul that survives death—a "ghost," as it was often called—tended to also believe that this essence would return, somehow, somewhere, in another body. This basic idea, once formed, grew deeper and more refined: from the belief in a single return to the idea of many lives; from the notion of fate to the understanding of karmic justice. And thus, through observation, reflection, and spiritual insight, humanity built a philosophy around three key realizations: that the soul survives death, that it has lived before, and that its future is shaped by its past.

Mystical traditions often add another dimension to this understanding. They claim that from time to time, humanity has been guided by advanced beings—Masters, Teachers, or Guides—who have outgrown the human cycle and now return to offer wisdom. Whether or not one accepts this, the undeniable fact remains: human beings, across time and culture, have again and again come to the same conclusion. We are more than bodies. We have lived before. And we will live again.

This belief has taken many forms. Ancient stone carvings and sacred symbols, uncovered by archaeologists like Soldi, speak of the universal belief in the soul's persistence. Many ancient peoples believed the soul would return to the body it left, which led to the practice of mummification and elaborate tomb rituals. But others moved beyond this idea and embraced a broader view: that the soul would inhabit new forms in new lifetimes.

From African tribes to Native American communities, early explorers recorded strange but familiar echoes of reincarnation—rituals, legends, and customs that suggested a belief in rebirth. In some societies, the bodies of deceased children were placed beside roads, with the hope that their souls might be drawn back to life through the bodies of women passing by. Some cultures believed in a layered soul—multiple spiritual components that functioned differently after death—an idea echoed in both ancient Hinduism and Chinese mysticism.

Among the Fijians, there was said to be a "black soul" that remained with the body and decayed with it, and a "white soul" that wandered and eventually reincarnated. Greenlandic natives believed in an astral body that left the sleeping form but died with the physical shell, alongside a more enduring soul that reincarnated. In nearly every region of the world, we find remnants of these layered beliefs, suggesting either a shared origin of thought—or a shared instinct among all people to seek continuity beyond death.

Even the fabled land of Atlantis, according to legend, cherished the idea of reincarnation and the soul's complexity. And if its descendants truly became the Egyptians and the ancient Peruvians, as some claim, then the continuity of this belief across oceans and centuries becomes easier to understand. Whether through inheritance or intuition, the thread remains unbroken: the soul journeys onward, life after life, drawn ever forward by the invisible hand of karma and the longing to return home.

Chapter II: Sacred Origins of Rebirth – Egypt, Chaldea, the Druids, and Beyond

As we move forward from our study of reincarnation among early tribal cultures and forgotten civilizations, we inevitably arrive at one of the most mystifying and spiritually charged regions of the ancient world—Egypt, the homeland of forgotten wisdom, mystical architecture, and sacred symbols. This land of pyramids and prophecy—where the silent Sphinx still stands guard—has long been associated with the most enduring spiritual teachings of humanity.

Whether the Egyptians were direct descendants of the legendary Atlanteans, as some esoteric traditions suggest, or simply a unique culture that reawakened ancient wisdom, the fact remains: when we follow the roots of any major occult or mystical doctrine, the path almost always leads us back to the banks of the Nile. The Sphinx itself seems to represent this truth—its sealed lips and enigmatic expression a metaphor for spiritual secrets held in waiting, revealed only to those whose inner ears are attuned to listen.

Despite its probable prehistoric origins, many scholars have argued that metempsychosis—that is, the soul's passage from one body to another—found one of its earliest structured expressions in ancient Egypt. Of course, this view is not without challenge; India, with its ancient spiritual traditions, also claims to be the birthplace of the reincarnation doctrine. And yet, because reincarnation remains a living, present-day belief in India, we will reserve that exploration for a later chapter focused on the modern era. For now, Egypt remains our focus—an ancient land where the idea of rebirth was woven deeply into the spiritual fabric of society.

Herodotus, writing in antiquity, recorded that the Egyptians were the first to formally propose the notion of an immortal soul. He described their belief that, upon death, the soul migrates to another body ready to receive it—moving through various earthly, aquatic, and aerial forms before eventually returning to the human experience. This soul journey, according to their teachings, spanned approximately three thousand years.

While the general population may have received a simplified or symbolic version of spiritual teachings, the deeper truths—such as reincarnation—were carefully guarded by the inner circle of priests and initiates. These mystical doctrines were preserved behind layers of ritual, symbol, and secrecy, shared only with those deemed ready. Still, fragments of these profound teachings occasionally reached the public, often through art, architecture, or ceremonial rites, and remain etched into stone and clay as echoes of a more complete inner knowledge.

Not only did the Egyptians uphold the belief in reincarnation, but they also developed one of the most sophisticated systems of esoteric philosophy the world has known. Their teachings described multiple layers of human existence—different aspects or "bodies" of the self. These included the **Ka** (the divine spark or spirit), **Ab** (will or intellect), **Hati** (vitality or life force), **Tet** (astral body), **Sahu** (the etheric double), and **Xa** (the physical form). Although various scholars differ slightly in how they categorize these components, the essential idea is the same: that humans are multidimensional beings, and only part of our nature is physical.

We find similar sophistication in the ancient **Chaldean** and **Persian** civilizations. Among them, the spiritual elite known as the **Magi**—renowned for their knowledge of astrology, alchemy, and sacred law—held reincarnation as a core truth. Unlike the Egyptians, whose masses often fell into idolatry, the Magi managed to maintain a higher level of purity in both their philosophy and religious expression, elevating the cultural understanding of the soul's journey.

The Magi taught that the human soul was not a single, indivisible unit, but rather a complex being composed of different parts—some temporary, others eternal. They believed that portions of the soul dissolved after death, while the most essential elements continued on, cycling through earthly and spiritual realms until reaching a state of inner perfection. Once this level of purity was attained, the soul would no longer need to reincarnate and would dwell in a realm of eternal light and peace.

Before entering this state of liberation, the soul, they taught, would pass through a moment of awakening —a panoramic review of all its former lives, seeing clearly the karmic threads that linked one incarnation to the next. Through this deep awareness, the soul would gain wisdom not just for itself but also in preparation for assisting future generations—serving as a guide, teacher, or helper for those still on the path of evolution.

The teachings of the Magi extended beyond humanity to include all existence. They believed that everything—living or seemingly inert—was an expression of the One Life. Therefore, true knowledge required recognizing the fundamental unity of all things and feeling a conscious sense of spiritual kinship with all forms of life, regardless of appearance or form.

Even in **ancient China**, beneath the layers of philosophical and religious formalism, one can detect clear traces of reincarnation. It appears in the teachings of great sages like **Lao-Tze**, whose influential text, the *Tao Te Ching*, remains a cornerstone of Eastern wisdom. While Lao-Tze's public teachings emphasized the flow of the Tao—the universal, unnameable source of all things—his inner circle received deeper initiations into the mysteries of the soul's immortality and return.

Lao-Tze spoke of the **Tao** as the primordial origin, and of the **Teh** as the dynamic force through which creation flows. From these arose all things, including the human soul, which he divided into spiritual and vital elements. The **huen** represented the ethereal, upward-bound aspect of the self, while the **phi** was associated with vitality and physical animation. He taught that ignorance of the soul's immortality was the cause of much suffering, and that understanding one's divine essence was essential for freedom. As he wrote: "What belongs to the earth shall return to the earth; what is of heaven shall ascend to heaven. Such is the Law."

While some later interpretations suggest he believed the soul immediately returned to the Tao after death, writings from his early disciples tell a different story. They suggest that the soul retained its individuality through many lifetimes, only merging with the Tao after its cycle of rebirth was complete. As stated in the *Si Haei*, "The spirit of knowing does not perish with the body. Though the vital forces dissolve, the soul remains, manifesting again by law."

The **Taoist** tradition also included a belief in karma—that actions in this life bore fruit in future existences. While Chinese religious systems created intricate models of heavens and hells to reflect this, the deeper, older teaching emphasized soul continuity and the spiritual consequences of every deed. Some systems described the soul as having three parts: the **kuei** (earthly soul, perishable with the body), the **ling** (an emotional-intellectual essence that survived for a time), and the **huen** (the immortal soul that journeyed through many lives). These layers of soul experience align with many mystical philosophies across the world.

Perhaps one of the more surprising discoveries for modern readers is that the **Druids**, the mysterious priesthood of ancient Gaul and Britain, also embraced a belief in reincarnation. Although often dismissed as barbarians, the Druids maintained a remarkably advanced spiritual philosophy that intertwined with their mystical form of worship and understanding of the cosmos.

The Roman conquerors, including Caesar and other classical writers, were frequently astonished by the depth and structure of Druidic knowledge. Later Christian figures—such as St. Clement and St. Cyril—also acknowledged their sophistication. Historian Reynaud observed that if Judea represented the monotheistic God, and Greece the development of social ideals, then Gaul—the Druidic stronghold—represented the deeply rooted belief in personal immortality and soul continuation.

Druidic teachings bore remarkable similarities to both the Egyptian mysteries and the Grecian initiatory schools, including those of **Hermetic** and **Pythagorean** origin. Though historical links between these groups have been lost, there are legends suggesting shared origins, mutual teachings, and spiritual alliances. Some claimed that **Pythagoras** himself taught the Druids, while others held that the Druidic order was influenced by **Zamolxis**, a disciple of Pythagoras who brought the teachings westward.

According to what survives of Druidic lore, they believed in a spiritual energy called **Awen**, a divine spark that flowed from the Universal Source and animated all life. This essence passed through all levels of existence—mineral, plant, animal—before reaching human form. The soul, trapped in cycles of dense material experience known as **Anufu**, eventually entered the **Circle of Abred**, the realm of human incarnation. Through growth and refinement, it could move into the **Circle of Bliss**, or **Gwynfid**, a state of spiritual joy and expanded consciousness. And beyond even that awaited **Ceugant**, the ultimate union with the Infinite—a concept strikingly similar to the Hindu *Nirvana* or the mystical *Union with God* described by the Persians and Greeks.

For a people so often labeled as primitive, this was a remarkably refined cosmology. It even surpassed the mythologies of their Roman conquerors in philosophical depth.

So respected was the Druidic understanding of death and rebirth that Gaulish society, under their guidance, implemented practices to reflect this spiritual perspective. For example, criminals sentenced to death were often granted a five-year delay for preparation—time to reflect, to purify, to ready the soul for its journey beyond this world. Such a custom reveals a powerful awareness of the soul's transition and the belief that one's state of mind at death influenced future incarnations.

It's important to understand that this spiritual depth did not necessarily reflect the average person's evolution, but rather the influence of the **Druidic priesthood**, who had inherited and preserved ancient knowledge. Traditions suggest that the original Druids came from distant lands—possibly Egypt or Greece—carrying with them sacred teachings and cosmic maps of the soul's journey. Their expertise in astronomy, ritual, and symbolic practice was legendary. Some of their customs echoed ancient Jewish rites, and even their beloved symbol—the **mistletoe**—was used to represent rebirth, as it grew anew from the sturdy oak.

The Druids left their mark across the British Isles and Ireland, not only through stone structures and ceremonial sites, but also in the folklore, superstitions, and oral traditions of the local people. Tales of fairies, ancestral spirits, and children who remembered past lives—all these stem from ancient Druidic seeds, passed down quietly through the generations.

Even now, whispers of those mystical truths remain, carried through the undercurrents of Celtic memory and spiritual intuition. They remind us that the soul does not forget—and that somewhere deep within, humanity remembers what it once knew: that life is a cycle, and we are eternal travelers through its sacred turns.

Chapter III: The Romans and the Greeks — Shadows of Thought and Echoes of Rebirth

To those unfamiliar with the deeper threads of spiritual philosophy, it might seem only natural to assume that the ancient Romans—renowned for their far-reaching power, their sprawling empire, and their enormous cultural influence—would also have developed sophisticated systems of metaphysics, spiritual doctrine, and esoteric insight. Considering their close political, military, and even artistic association with ancient Greece—one of the most intellectually vibrant civilizations of the past—it would be reasonable to expect that such spiritual or philosophical insights had flowed freely between them. But when we look more closely, we discover something surprisingly different.

While the Roman Empire did, indeed, borrow heavily from Greek religious forms, adapting the Greek gods under new Latin names and integrating Greek art, literature, and architecture into their own culture, their relationship with deeper metaphysical thought was relatively shallow. Their resemblance to Greek religion was mostly surface-level and aesthetic—rituals, temples, and tales—but the intellectual and mystical undercurrents were rarely adopted with the same depth or passion. The Romans, as a people, were far more focused on order, conquest, law, and civic engineering than they were on the mysteries of the soul, the journey of the afterlife, or the fate of human consciousness beyond the grave.

Their general outlook on life leaned heavily toward material achievement, tangible results, and earthly power. The intricacies of the spirit—immortality, karma, rebirth—were topics that rarely stirred the Roman imagination. Among the general population, there was little enthusiasm for engaging in abstract speculation about the soul's journey or the moral mechanics of the universe. And while a few exceptional individuals within Roman society did express interest in immortality and posthumous existence, such expressions were relatively isolated, and rarely reflected the dominant cultural ethos.

Take, for example, **Cicero**, whose writings do include fleeting insights into the notion of a soul that outlives the body. In his *"Dream of Scipio,"* he wrote words that suggest a higher vision of human nature: "Know that it is not you, but your body alone, which is mortal. The true person—the essence—is your soul. You, as immortal intelligence, are what animates this temporary frame of flesh, just as the eternal God gives motion to the universe." Cicero's statement stands out as luminous amid a sea of spiritual indifference. He recognized the soul as something godlike, distinct from the decaying vessel of the body.

Similarly, **Pliny the Younger** hinted in his writings at a belief in the existence of spirits or phantoms—entities that seemed to transcend death and linger in mysterious forms. **Ovid**, the poet of transformation, also crafted verses suggesting that some part of man lives on, beyond physical death. He mused that souls, having undergone refinement through good conduct, might evolve upward through a kind of spiritual chain, eventually becoming human in form. Yet even with such isolated expressions, Roman culture as a whole maintained only a lukewarm relationship with these mystical ideas.

Philosophically speaking, the Romans never developed a comprehensive spiritual system of their own. The idea of life after death was entertained as a possibility, sometimes explored through poetry or symbolic stories, but it was rarely embraced as a foundational truth. For many Roman thinkers, belief in immortality was more a poetic sentiment than a rational conclusion. It represented a longing for justice, a romantic echo of the human desire for meaning beyond death—but not something provable or worth staking doctrine upon.

Indeed, there were Roman intellectuals like **Lucretius** who actively spoke out against the belief in an afterlife. In his epic poem *De Rerum Natura* (On the Nature of Things), Lucretius strongly argued that the soul dies with the body, and that fear of an eternal afterlife only causes unnecessary anxiety and robs people of peace and happiness in their current existence. To him, eternity was not a promise but a threat—a superstition to be abandoned in favor of rational materialism.

Virgil, another Roman poet, admired those who possessed the courage and clarity of vision to reject the "irrational fears" of divine judgment and posthumous punishment. In his writings, he praised the philosophical attitude that sought to understand the natural order of things and thereby dismiss the need for dread about what might follow death. And yet, paradoxically, some of these very same thinkers who rejected the soul's survival still believed in supernatural forces, omens, and divine signs—revealing an odd blend of rationalism and superstition within Roman thought.

So we find the Roman worldview curiously inconsistent. On one hand, they exhibited skepticism toward reincarnation and metaphysical continuity; on the other, they maintained rituals and customs that acknowledged invisible realms. There was an element of ancestor veneration, for instance, in which the spirits of the deceased were believed to continue in some way—albeit not through reincarnation. But this practice was more social than spiritual, more about family honor and household tradition than about metaphysical belief in soul evolution.

This ancestor worship took the form of rituals aimed at pleasing or honoring the collective "soul" of one's forebears. The idea was not that individual ancestors returned in new bodies, but that their essence had somehow merged into a larger familial spirit, or ancestral presence, which protected the lineage. Offerings were made, not from theological conviction, but out of a sense of duty to one's heritage and the fear of social dishonor.

In spite of the general spiritual apathy, there were occasional Roman figures who flirted with reincarnationist thought. **Ovid**, for example, wrote: "Nothing truly perishes; everything transforms. The soul journeys endlessly, assuming visible forms; animals that become good may rise to the level of man." **Virgil**, too, hinted at a cyclical cosmology. He imagined that, after judgment in the Elysian Fields or Tartarus, souls would drink from the waters of **Lethe**, which would erase their memories, preparing them for new lives back on Earth.

Still, it would be fair to conclude that Rome, as a civilization, did not engage deeply with the concept of reincarnation. Their gaze was turned outward—toward conquest, law, and the building of empire—rather than inward, toward spiritual rebirth or transcendence. In contrast, their neighbors and philosophical predecessors, the **Greeks**, nurtured a far richer and more profound exploration of the soul's journey and its many lifetimes.

The ancient Greeks, though divided among many schools of thought, were far more invested in metaphysical questions, particularly those concerning the immortality and evolution of the soul. While the common Greek citizen may have been content with mythological stories and public rituals honoring Zeus or Athena, there was always a thriving undercurrent of deep philosophical inquiry. The intellectual class—composed of sages, poets, philosophers, and mystics—delved earnestly into the questions of existence, purpose, and the continuity of consciousness.

Alongside the Hindus, the Greeks can rightfully be considered one of the most philosophically gifted cultures in human history. Their legacy shaped Western thought for centuries and continues to influence modern spiritual seekers. Within their cultural landscape, the doctrine of reincarnation—known more precisely as metempsychosis—occupied a central place in many spiritual and philosophical systems.

Though diverse in their views, Greek thinkers often converged on one basic principle: the soul is immortal and is subject to a cosmic law that governs its return to the earthly realm. Those souls who lived wisely and purely might escape the cycle of rebirth, ascending to realms of eternal peace, while others—having lived selfishly or ignorantly—would pass through the waters of **Lethe**, drink its potion of forgetfulness, and be reborn to continue their spiritual education.

One of the **Orphic hymns**, attributed to the mystical followers of **Orpheus**, expresses this clearly: "The wise seek light, not darkness. As you journey through life, never forget the journey's end. When souls return to the divine light, they carry upon their subtler bodies the stains and scars of past transgressions. These must be cleansed, and the soul must return to Earth for purification. But the noble and the virtuous ascend immediately to the radiant presence of Dionysus." This belief system echoes the Egyptian tradition of soul evolution and carries with it the same tone of mystical urgency and spiritual refinement.

Among the Greeks, one figure stands above all others in shaping the philosophical foundation of reincarnation: **Pythagoras**. Known to history primarily as a mathematician, Pythagoras was far more than that—he was an occult teacher, a spiritual reformer, and the founder of a secret initiatory school devoted to soul development and cosmic harmony. Pythagoras taught that the soul passed through many lifetimes, inhabiting various forms according to the moral and spiritual nature of its previous deeds.

Though much of his wisdom was reserved for the initiates of his mystery school, he made public certain teachings on the nature of the soul's journey. His doctrines bear strong resemblance to both Hindu and Egyptian thought. He described the human being as composed of multiple "bodies" or sheaths—some perishable, others immortal. After death, the higher soul would journey to a realm of light, receive spiritual insight, commune with advanced beings, and prepare for its next incarnation. Only once the soul achieved a certain level of perfection could it break the cycle and reside permanently in bliss.

According to **Pythagoras**, the circumstances of one's rebirth—status, intelligence, fortune—were not random but were determined by one's actions and character in previous lives. This teaching mirrors the doctrine of karma and reinforces the principle of divine justice at work in the cosmos. He asserted that this doctrine explained why human lives are so unequal—why some are born into privilege and others into hardship. It was not fate or the whims of the gods, but the just result of past causes.

He also held that, while the material world operated under mechanical laws of necessity, there existed a higher, spiritual order that transcended those laws. The soul, in its journey upward, could eventually access this higher order and operate in harmony with it, becoming a co-creator in the unfolding of divine will.

Following in his footsteps, the immortal **Plato**—perhaps the greatest philosopher of the Western world—deepened and refined the doctrine of reincarnation. In his works, especially *Phaedo*, *Republic*, and *Timaeus*, Plato presents a vision of the soul's journey that is both poetic and metaphysically rigorous. He taught that each soul, upon death, must account for its deeds and then either ascend to a higher realm, descend into purification, or return to Earth for another incarnation.

Plato believed that the soul retained, in subtle form, impressions and intuitions from its past lives. These manifested as *innate ideas*—instinctive knowledge of beauty, truth, and goodness—that guided the soul even if conscious memory was erased. He wrote that the soul is immortal, divine in origin, and subject to growth through the experience of many lives. He compared its journey to that of a traveler ascending a spiral path, each lifetime representing another step toward reunion with the Supreme Source.

In Plato's metaphysics, the soul had a tripartite structure. The highest aspect was **Spirit**—intelligence, will, moral choice—anchored in the head. Below that was the **passionate soul**, seated in the heart, associated with courage, desire, and emotion. Lastly, the **appetitive soul**, located in the lower body, governed instinct, craving, and sensual drive. The higher aspect was eternal; the lower ones were mortal and prone to dissolution, though capable of influencing the soul's development and karmic record.

The **Neo-Platonists**, who came after Plato, including **Plotinus** and **Porphyry**, embraced and elaborated on reincarnation as part of their mystical cosmology. They developed refined theories of soul evolution, divine emanation, and spiritual purification. Their work blended Greek, Egyptian, and even Eastern ideas into a unified mystical philosophy that influenced early Christianity, especially through the **Essenes**, a Jewish sect known for their belief in reincarnation and their mystical lifestyle.

In truth, Plato's influence echoes far beyond his own era. His writings prepared the way for deeper spiritual understanding throughout Western civilization. Many of the early **Christian Fathers** viewed him as a kind of prophetic figure—a pagan voice speaking divine truths ahead of Christ. His vision of the immortal soul, journeying through time in pursuit of perfection, still resonates today as a central archetype in the human search for meaning.

Chapter IV: The Jews, the Essenes, and the Early Christians — Hidden Threads of Rebirth

Among the early Hebrew people, there existed a layered spiritual tradition—an *Inner Teaching* known only to a select few—which contained ideas that closely resembled the doctrine of reincarnation. While the masses remained unaware of such teachings, a smaller, more spiritually educated group preserved and transmitted these esoteric truths, often in secrecy. The surface religion of ancient Israel, as recorded in their scriptures and practiced in the temple, made little mention of the soul's journey beyond death. However, deeper currents flowed beneath the surface, visible to those who knew where to look.

Scholars and historians have long debated the nature of early Jewish beliefs regarding the afterlife. Many agree that, in its earliest form, Jewish theology offered only a vague and shadowy vision of what happens after death. In the early books of the Hebrew Bible—especially the Pentateuch—there is little discussion of the soul's fate beyond the grave. The general belief of the people centered around a gloomy, subterranean realm called **Sheol**, a dark and silent place where all souls, regardless of virtue or vice, were said to dwell in a state of unconscious sleep. It was not heaven, nor hell—more like an eternal shadow.

However, over time, we can observe a subtle but significant shift in thought. As the Jewish people came into contact with other cultures—especially during their exile and their time in **Egypt**—their conception of the soul began to evolve. It's highly likely that the educated class within ancient Israel, though small in number due to the social conditions of bondage and oppression, absorbed elements of Egyptian mystical teachings. **Moses** himself, raised and educated among the Egyptian elite, almost certainly encountered the sacred rites and metaphysical doctrines of Egypt's priesthood. According to Jewish tradition, Moses created an inner circle of spiritual leaders after leading his people out of Egypt, and many believe he passed down to them the esoteric knowledge he had acquired—knowledge too advanced and symbolic to be taught to the general population of the time, who were largely unprepared for such depth.

Through the centuries, various Jewish sages and mystics have spoken—often obliquely—of a **Secret Teaching** hidden behind the public face of Judaism. Many **rabbis** and spiritual authorities have hinted at this inner tradition, and several early **Christian Fathers** acknowledged its possible existence, suggesting that Judaism contained a dual-layered theology: one for the masses, and one for the initiated.

Linguistic and textual scholars have also noted something telling in the **language** of the Old Testament. In the original Hebrew texts, three distinct words are used when referring to the immaterial aspect of the human being: **"Neshamah"**, **"Ruach"**, and **"Nephesh."** While later translators often rendered all three as "soul" or "spirit," their original meanings suggest a more complex structure. Many respected interpreters believe these terms denote separate spiritual components, much like the trifold conception of the soul found in **Egyptian, Chaldean, and Greek** mysticism. In this interpretation, *Neshamah* corresponds to the **Ego** or Higher Self—the divine, intelligent principle; *Ruach* is the subtle vehicle or mental-emotional body; and *Nephesh* relates to **vital energy**, the animating life force that sustains the physical organism.

Perhaps the richest and most detailed account of soul doctrine within the Jewish tradition is found in the **Kabbalah**—the ancient, esoteric body of mystical literature that serves as a key to understanding the hidden dimensions of scripture and spirit. The **Kabbalah**, which means "received tradition," speaks in the language of **symbol and allegory**, requiring specialized knowledge to unlock its secrets. For the uninitiated, its cryptic verses may seem meaningless, even chaotic. But to those who hold the "keys," the Kabbalah reveals profound insights into the structure of the universe, the nature of divinity, and the soul's evolutionary journey.

One of the central ideas in Kabbalistic teaching is the **multi-layered nature of the soul**. It distinguishes clearly between Neshamah, Ruach, and Nephesh, seeing them as distinct energetic layers that work together during incarnation and separate after death. The **Zohar**, the most celebrated mystical text within Kabbalistic literature (though of later origin than the Kabbalah itself), expands on these themes and introduces a striking view of **reincarnation**—or **gilgul**, as it is sometimes called in Hebrew.

According to the Zohar, when a soul leaves the body, it does not immediately ascend into the divine presence. Instead, it undergoes a long and sometimes arduous process of purification. The effects of past misdeeds—be they selfishness, cruelty, or spiritual ignorance—must be cleansed through **multiple lifetimes** and spiritual trials. The soul is drawn back into physical incarnation not as punishment per se, but as an opportunity for learning, refinement, and ultimately, **union with the divine**.

Whereas **Plato** emphasized rebirth as a form of consequence or karma, the Jewish mystical tradition tends to frame reincarnation more as a method of **soul-completion**—a process through which all the latent divine potentials within the soul must be awakened and fulfilled. Until that fulfillment occurs, the soul returns to the physical world over and over again, often in complete amnesia of its former lives, but driven by an inner urge to evolve.

A striking passage from the Zohar summarizes this beautifully:

"All souls are subject to the trials of transmigration; and men do not know the ways of the Most High. They do not know how many transformations and hidden trials await them. Many souls come into this world, yet do not return to the palace of the divine King. The soul must eventually return to the Source from which it came. But this reunion cannot occur until it has developed all the virtues, the seeds of which are planted in it from the beginning. If this is not completed in one life, it must return again, and again, until it is ready."

Perhaps the most well-known mystical group within Jewish history—particularly in the centuries leading up to the birth of Christ—was the order of the **Essenes**. This group, often described as an ascetic and contemplative sect, played a crucial role in preserving and transmitting the doctrine of reincarnation. Active in Palestine and particularly near the **Dead Sea**, the Essenes formed a community that combined Egyptian mysticism, Greek philosophy (especially Pythagorean and Platonic), and Jewish spiritual traditions.

The **Jewish historian Josephus** described the Essenes with great respect. He wrote:

"They believe that the body is corruptible, and its matter not eternal. But the soul, coming from the most refined ether, is immortal. The soul is imprisoned in the body like a captive in chains. When freed, it rejoices and ascends to the heavenly realms."

Other historical references, such as the *New International Encyclopedia*, confirm this portrayal. It notes that the Essenes believed the soul to be **pre-existent**, and that its entrapment in the body was a temporary trial—a crucible through which it must pass in order to evolve. The encyclopedia also highlights the remarkable **parallels between the Essenes and early Christianity**, especially in their emphasis on righteousness, purity, and **baptism**—ritual cleansing by water, which was central to their way of life.

Indeed, many researchers have drawn a strong connection between the Essenes and **John the Baptist**, suggesting that he either trained with or was influenced by their teachings. His life in the wilderness, his call for inner transformation, and his focus on ethical rebirth all align closely with Essene values. While it's debated whether **Jesus himself** had direct ties to this group, it is undeniable that the early Christian movement was shaped by the same mystical currents that flowed through the Essenes and their contemporaries.

That brings us naturally to the next significant evolution of the reincarnation doctrine—its presence in the **early Christian Church**. While modern Christianity is largely silent on the topic, a careful examination of early Church history reveals that **an Inner Doctrine** did exist, and that it included belief in the **pre-existence of the soul** and its journey through multiple lives.

The writings of **Paul** and other early apostles often allude to *Mysteries*—hidden truths meant only for the spiritually mature. In several of Paul's epistles, he differentiates between milk for the babes in faith and meat for the spiritually initiated—language suggesting two levels of instruction: **exoteric** (public) and **esoteric** (private). This structure mirrored the mystery schools of Egypt, Greece, and even ancient Israel.

Celsus, a critic of Christianity in the second century, accused the early Church of being a **secretive cult** that taught its deeper doctrines only to a chosen few, while offering the masses watered-down allegories and moral tales. In response, the Church Father **Origen** acknowledged that this was indeed the case—but not in a negative sense. Origen argued that all true spiritual traditions made a distinction between the outer teaching and the inner mysteries, and that Christianity was simply following that timeless precedent.

In his rebuttal, Origen stated:

"That there are doctrines not made known to the multitude, but only disclosed after the basic teachings have been taught, is not a peculiar practice of Christianity. It is also found in all philosophical systems, including that of Pythagoras. Even among the Greeks and 'barbarian' nations, sacred truths are revealed only to those who are prepared to receive them."

In another passage, Origen cryptically remarks:

"It is good to keep secret the mystery of the king," referring to the belief that the soul's descent into the body should not be discussed openly, lest it be misunderstood or degraded by the unprepared.

Dozens of similar quotations can be found in the writings of early Church leaders, pointing to an inner circle that quietly upheld teachings such as **reincarnation, pre-existence**, and the **soul's gradual return to its**

divine source. Origen himself, considered one of the most brilliant minds of the early Church, wrote extensively about these themes. He taught that all souls began in a pure state of unity with God and that through misuse of free will, they descended into physical incarnation. From that point on, the soul's journey became one of **return**, through successive lives, toward the divine.

Justin Martyr, another early Christian writer, also hinted at the idea of the soul inhabiting successive bodies, while **Lactantius** stated that immortality implies pre-existence. Even **St. Augustine**, who often disagreed with Origen, once wrote in his *Confessions*:

"Did I not live in another body before entering my mother's womb?"

Yet despite these echoes, reincarnation slowly fell out of favor within mainstream Christianity. As Church councils began to exert more control over doctrine, the mystical teachings were labeled as **heresy**. In 538 A.D., under the rule of **Justinian**, a formal condemnation was issued:

"Whoever supports the mythical notion of the soul's pre-existence or its return after death, let him be anathema."

But spiritual ideas do not perish so easily. Although suppressed by institutional decree, the **flame of reincarnation** continued to burn quietly. For centuries it lingered in the margins—hidden in poetry, mysticism, secret orders, and the personal beliefs of independent thinkers. During the Renaissance and Enlightenment periods, it began to rise again, slowly reclaiming its place in the evolving spiritual consciousness of the West.

By the **nineteenth and twentieth centuries**, the doctrine of reincarnation experienced a full-scale **revival**, embraced by both esoteric schools and everyday seekers. Today, thousands of individuals once again study, teach, and meditate upon the soul's great journey—not as a foreign or exotic idea, but as a **universal truth** remembered.

Chapter V: India – Cradle of the Soul's Journey

Although the belief in reincarnation has surfaced across a wide variety of ancient cultures and civilizations, both past and present, India remains the land most deeply rooted in this doctrine. We may rightly consider it the natural birthplace of the idea, not necessarily because it originated there, but because the concept has found such a receptive and enduring spiritual environment among its people. The origin of the teaching in India is so ancient that it lies buried in the mists of prehistory, and yet the philosophy remains alive, not merely as a relic of the past, but as a living, evolving truth. In India, the tree of reincarnation continues to flourish, bearing fruits for those who seek spiritual understanding in the modern world.

Hindu scholars proudly assert that long before the modern Western world emerged from its primitive roots—before even the ancient Hebrews had laid the foundation for their religious systems—India had already developed a profound metaphysical framework. The sages and philosophers of India had not only recognized but also refined the principles of reincarnation, embedding them into a vast and intricate philosophical system. The teachings were not merely religious beliefs but formed a comprehensive worldview adopted by the Aryan race in India and preserved through thousands of years. Through countless generations—spanning over four millennia—this tradition has endured, passed down with reverence and faith, surviving changing political landscapes and cultural transformations. Now, as the spiritual hunger in the West grows, many thoughtful minds are turning eastward, seeking in the wisdom of the Vedas and Upanishads the spiritual antidote to the widespread disillusionment of materialism.

While nearly every religious and philosophical system in history has, at one point or another, flirted with the idea of reincarnation, it is only in India that the concept has blossomed to its fullest extent. In Indian thought, past and present, the notion of soul migration has been central, not peripheral. From the earliest moments of its spiritual life, the Indian mind has embraced the idea that human beings are more than their physical form. This belief permeates every facet of Hindu life and culture—even today, nearly all Hindus accept reincarnation as a foundational truth. With the exception of Indian Muslims, whose views are influenced by Islam, virtually every subdivision of the Hindu population—from different castes to philosophical sects—regards reincarnation as self-evident. It is not an abstract theory to be debated, but a lived reality.

To the typical Hindu, the soul is not something the body owns or carries, but rather the opposite: the body is a temporary vessel housing the eternal self. This subtle but powerful distinction defines the Hindu worldview. The body is transient, one of many forms adopted by the soul in its long journey through countless lifetimes. This current life, with all its dramas and sorrows, is but a single step in an infinite stairway of experience. Eternity is not some far-off reward—it is already unfolding around and within us. The Hindu recognizes that he lives in eternity now, just as he always has and always will. Each incarnation is but a brief act in the grand theater of existence.

The original religious expression of the early Hindus was not encumbered with the layers of complexity seen in modern times. There were no rigid creeds or elaborate rituals in those early days. Their religion was, in essence, a kind of elevated nature-worship, though the term fails to capture the profound spiritual depth it embodied. Nature, to the ancient Hindu, was not just a collection of elements or natural forces—it was alive, infused with Spirit. Behind every form, every event, every life, there pulsed a singular divine energy, a universal consciousness expressing itself through infinite manifestations.

Even at this early stage, reincarnation was present as a foundational concept. Though they saw all life as expressions of one Divine Reality, the soul was understood as a distinct, evolving spark—emerging from the One Life, diverging for a time through various incarnations, and ultimately destined to return to unity with the Divine. This journey was not a punishment or test, but a process of refinement, a slow unfolding of consciousness toward its source. Over the centuries, this foundational idea gave rise to a multitude of philosophies, schools, and religious movements. Yet despite the immense variety in outward practice, the inner thread of reincarnation remained intact.

The development of Brahmanism was a significant evolution in Indian religious thought. It began with simple philosophical notions, which gradually became surrounded by complex theological structures, ceremonial customs, and metaphysical abstractions. A powerful priesthood emerged, systematizing rituals and interpreting doctrines in increasingly sophisticated ways. In time, Buddhism rose as a kind of response—an attempt to return to the simplicity of spiritual truth. However, Buddhism too developed its own systems, schools, and hierarchies. Still, through every transformation and reinterpretation, the belief in reincarnation never lost its central place. It remained the unshakable foundation upon which Indian metaphysical thought was built.

The ancient texts of India are overflowing with references to reincarnation. The Laws of Manu—among the oldest Sanskrit writings—are rich with mention of soul rebirth. The Vedas and Upanishads offer countless passages that affirm the transmigration of the soul. And perhaps nowhere is the doctrine more beautifully stated than in the Bhagavad Gita. There, the deity Krishna, speaking to the warrior Arjuna, proclaims:

"Know this, O Prince, that there never was a time when I, you, or any of these assembled kings did not exist; nor shall there ever come a time when any of us shall cease to be. Just as the soul experiences childhood, youth, and old age through the same body, so too will it pass into another body after death. The wise grieve not for this transition."

Krishna goes further, explaining that the soul is not touched by birth or death. The true self is eternal, uncreated, and undying. Death affects only the outer garment—the body—which, like old clothes, is cast off and replaced by new ones. The soul, he declares, continues unharmed, beyond the reach of sword, fire, or time itself. In Krishna's words: "As a man discards worn garments and dons new ones, so the soul sheds a worn-out body and enters another, fresh and ready." He reminds Arjuna that though we may forget our past lives, they are not lost. "You have lived many lives," Krishna says, "as have I. But while I remember them all, you remember none."

This teaching appears repeatedly across India's vast body of spiritual literature. The Mahabharata echoes the metaphor of discarded clothing, emphasizing that the soul leaves behind its old forms and enters new ones, avoiding the pitfalls of error and continuing its journey toward heaven or liberation. The Brhadaranyaka Upanishad offers yet another poetic image: as a caterpillar, reaching the end of a leaf, reaches forward and draws itself onward, so too the soul, having found a new place, withdraws from its current body and continues forward. Like a goldsmith who melts and reshapes metal into new ornaments, the soul fashions for itself a new dwelling, made fit for the next phase of its journey.

To attempt a full compilation of reincarnation references from Indian scriptures would require entire libraries. So deeply embedded is the idea that, without it, Indian spirituality would lose its essence. One might say that to remove reincarnation from these texts would be like presenting the play of Hamlet without Hamlet himself.

A detailed examination of all the Hindu religious schools is beyond the scope of this chapter. The sheer variety of sects, lineages, and philosophical systems would require volumes to explore. Yet beneath this surface diversity lies a shared vision: that all living beings emerge from a single divine source—an infinite consciousness that manifests in countless individual forms. These souls, born into material existence, often forget their true nature. Enveloped in ignorance (avidya), they mistake the world of form (maya) for reality. And so begins the long spiral of rebirth, each life an opportunity for growth and realization. Through the cycles of karma and reincarnation, the soul gradually sheds illusion, awakening to its essence and eventually merging back into the divine totality.

This spiritual ascent—this climb from forgetfulness to realization—is viewed differently by various schools, but the underlying structure remains the same. Some focus on metaphysical classifications, dividing the self into seven sheaths or layers, progressing from the most gross to the most subtle. These are:

1. The physical body (Rupa)
2. The life force or vitality (Prana-Jiva)
3. The astral or etheric double (Linga Sharira)
4. The animal or emotional soul (Kama Rupa)
5. The rational or human soul (Manas)
6. The spiritual soul (Buddhi)
7. The divine essence or spirit (Atma)

Though terminology may vary among schools, this layered model of the self is commonly accepted as a map of human consciousness. The soul progresses by shedding each lower layer, moving toward greater purity and unity with its divine origin.

From the earliest times, Hindu philosophers sought to understand not just the external world, but the deep structure of consciousness itself. While modern science in the West asks "How?", the ancient Indian mind asked "Why?" This inward-turning gaze birthed a host of sophisticated systems, all aimed at understanding the soul's place in the cosmos. Whether they favored devotional practice, intellectual analysis, or yogic discipline, Hindu philosophers universally returned to one idea: the soul is evolving, lifetime after lifetime, toward a return to its divine source.

And so, India remains not merely a land of temples and myths, but a vast spiritual laboratory—one that has, for thousands of years, charted the map of the soul's journey. In that sacred soil, reincarnation is not theory—it is experience, encoded in the culture, embedded in every ritual, and etched into the collective memory of a people who see life not as a beginning or end, but as a circle without boundary.

CHAPTER VI – Reincarnation in the Modern West

In recent decades, the concept of reincarnation has surged into the collective consciousness of the Western world with surprising force. While once regarded as a mystical Eastern doctrine, today it finds itself a frequent subject in philosophical discussions, novels, poems, plays, and even mainstream magazine features. Over the past century, and particularly within the last two decades, the public's curiosity and engagement with the idea has increased dramatically. This isn't merely a trend or intellectual curiosity—it represents a deeper hunger for spiritual continuity and meaning in life, beyond the confines of a single earthly existence.

This renewed attention can be attributed to the broader Western fascination with mysticism, spiritual philosophy, comparative religion, and the ancient teachings of the East. A significant moment came in 1893 during the World's Parliament of Religions, held at the Chicago World's Fair, which brought Eastern spiritual teachers to the attention of Western audiences. Yet perhaps no influence was more instrumental than the work of the Theosophical Society—founded by the enigmatic Madame Blavatsky in the late 19th century. Through books, lectures, and the magnetism of spiritual personalities, Theosophy kindled Western interest in reincarnation and presented it in a structured, systematic way.

Regardless of its origin, reincarnation has now become a vital part of Western philosophical and spiritual thought. Even those who do not fully embrace the doctrine find it increasingly difficult to ignore. It has re-entered the mainstream with a force that compels examination.

However, as in the East, the interpretations and expressions of reincarnation vary widely in the West. Some gravitate toward the Hindu model, often through the lens of Theosophy or Yogi teachings. Others are drawn to Platonic or Egyptian perspectives, particularly within Western occult circles that operate quietly, appealing to a select group of spiritual aspirants rather than the general public. There are also many Christians who reinterpret their faith through the concept of rebirth, harking back to early Gnostic and Neo-Platonic teachings within the Church.

The Theosophical framework offers one of the most detailed and widely circulated explanations of reincarnation in the West. It portrays the human soul as a composite made up of seven distinct layers or "principles," which are:

1. The Physical Body (Rupa)
2. The Vital Force (Prana-Jiva)
3. The Astral Body (Linga-Sharira)
4. The Animal Soul (Kama-Rupa)
5. The Human Soul (Manas)
6. The Spiritual Soul (Buddhi)
7. The Spirit (Atma)

According to this model, the lower four principles perish upon death, while the higher triad—Manas, Buddhi, and Atma—continues. These surviving elements, known as the Higher Self, embark on further spiritual journeys, shedding temporary forms and evolving toward union with higher planes of being.

Theosophy also introduces the idea of the "Life Wave," a great stream of Egos or Monads traveling through a sequence of seven planetary globes—known as the Planetary Chain—on a vast spiral journey of evolution. Each globe represents a distinct stage of development, and within each globe, the soul moves through seven root races, each with seven sub-races and seven branch races. Earth, according to this model, is currently experiencing its fourth cycle, with humanity in the fifth root race of that cycle. Between incarnations, the soul rests in Devachan, a kind of celestial retreat, the duration of which depends on its spiritual progress. It is said that most souls reincarnate after a rest of roughly 1,500 years.

Another influential stream in Western reincarnation thought is the Yogi Philosophy, which shares much with its Indian roots but has adapted to Western sensibilities. Unlike Theosophy, the Yogi system does not crystallize into any formal organization. It instead spreads through books and teachings that reach thousands of independent students.

Yogi Philosophy views the Universe as a mental projection of the Absolute—unfolding first through involution (spirit descending into matter) and then evolving back toward spiritual awareness. In this paradigm, souls are seen as sparks of divine consciousness undergoing experience and refinement through a grand evolutionary process. This path, while long and complex, is understood as leading inexorably toward reunion with the Infinite Source.

The Yogi system also recognizes seven aspects of the human being:

1. Physical Body
2. Astral Body
3. Vital Force (Prana)
4. Instinctive Mind
5. Intellect
6. Spiritual Mind
7. Spirit

The lower four are transient, while the higher three persist and reincarnate. The Yogi model emphasizes not only spiritual growth, but also the importance of conscious reincarnation, where a soul may one day retain memory across lives. Karma, in this framework, is seen less as retributive justice and more as a law of spiritual causation, in which desire and attraction shape future conditions.

While many reincarnationists lean toward Hindu or Yogi teachings, others are drawn more to Platonic or early Christian mysticism. Among these are "Spiritists," who view the Spirit as the true, eternal self. They propose that reincarnation is a process of development from primitive life forms, through successive human lives, and eventually to god-like states of being across multiple universes. They do not stress the exact number of soul layers, considering such details secondary to the core reality that the soul progresses ever upward toward divine union.

There also exists a quieter group of seekers—those influenced by ancient Greco-Egyptian and Neo-Platonic thought—who gather in small esoteric circles rather than large public movements. These groups believe that human existence is part of a great "descent into matter," a Fall from spiritual unity into physical limitation. Reincarnation, in this view, is a return journey—an attempt to rediscover divine origin, the "Father's house," as expressed allegorically in the parable of the Prodigal Son. Earth is considered a realm halfway between spiritual darkness and light, and the soul's work is to climb upward through its own striving.

Another category of believers may surprise many: those within the Christian Church. Quietly and often privately, many Christians have begun to explore reincarnation as compatible with their faith. They prefer the term "rebirth" to avoid association with what they consider non-Christian roots. These Christians see rebirth as a means of spiritual redemption and development—a second (or third, or tenth) chance for the soul to evolve and enter the heavenly realm. Heaven itself, in this view, is a place of continuous growth rather than static bliss.

This vision of eternal progression echoes through many streams of reincarnation philosophy. It stands in contrast to the traditional Christian view of a single life followed by eternal reward or punishment. For these Christian reincarnationists, the idea of spiritual advancement beyond this world brings comfort, hope, and purpose. Their beliefs echo the early church fathers and mystics who once held similar views, long before ecclesiastical councils dismissed them as heresy.

It's worth noting that this revival of interest in reincarnation may itself be a product of reincarnation. Some modern occult teachers suggest that many individuals in Europe and America today are reborn souls from ancient civilizations—Indians, Egyptians, Greeks, or early Christians—now returning with renewed interest in the doctrines they once held dear. Thus, those now drawn to Hindu, Greek, or Gnostic interpretations may simply be continuing a soul journey they began millennia ago.

In the end, despite the many forms and philosophies, the central thread remains the same: life is not a single chapter, but a long narrative. The soul is not a momentary flicker, but an eternal flame seeking to burn ever more brightly. Reincarnation, in all its variations, is an affirmation that nothing is wasted—that all experience, joy, sorrow, error, and triumph—contributes to the soul's unfolding destiny.

Chapter VII: Between and Beyond Lives – The Journey of the Soul

One of the most frequently asked questions by those newly introduced to the study of reincarnation is this: "Where does the soul go between lives? Does reincarnation happen immediately after death? And ultimately, where is the final resting place or goal of the soul?" These questions have echoed across centuries and civilizations, and even in our modern era, they remain deeply significant to any serious student of metaphysical thought. While countless teachers and philosophers have offered differing responses, we will now examine the most respected and enduring perspectives on the matter.

Let us first address the fundamental query: "Does the soul reincarnate immediately after physical death?" Early thinkers in reincarnation offered a variety of answers. Some taught that reincarnation happened quickly, with the soul returning to a new body after only a brief interlude during which it rebalanced its energies, resolved character-based tendencies, and prepared for a new cycle of experience. According to these early views, this transitional stage was used to mentally process the last lifetime, reflect on its moral choices, and prepare to correct past mistakes—especially since the soul, unburdened by material distractions, could now perceive its spiritual nature more clearly. This period of reflection offered the soul a broader perspective, from which it could better judge what truly matters in human existence.

In contrast, modern spiritual schools tend to agree that the average interval between incarnations spans approximately fifteen hundred years. However, this duration is not fixed. Less evolved souls—those who are still deeply immersed in material desires and instinctual impulses—are said to return more quickly, often within a few years or decades. Their brief time in the spiritual realm corresponds with their inability to sustain higher states of consciousness. These souls are pulled rapidly back into incarnation by their lingering cravings for physical pleasures, attachments, and unfinished business.

Indeed, such earthbound souls often find opportunities to reincarnate with relative ease. Families of similar temperament and vibration are believed to attract such souls, offering appropriate bodies and life circumstances that mirror the soul's previous tendencies. On the other hand, more advanced souls, having cultivated deeper spiritual insight and refined their character, enjoy longer periods between incarnations. They linger in the higher planes of being, taking time to contemplate, rest, and grow before re-entering the cycle of birth. Some accounts suggest that spiritually awakened souls may remain in these higher states for thousands—even tens of thousands—of years unless they willingly return sooner to assist in humanity's upliftment.

Moreover, according to certain advanced teachings, such awakened souls do not lose consciousness upon reincarnating. Instead, they retain memory of their past lives and consciously choose the conditions into which they are reborn. This selective reincarnation is thought to be impossible for souls still caught in lower levels of awareness, as such individuals are not yet ready for the responsibility of choosing their path.

Next, we face a more intricate question: "Where does the soul reside between incarnations?" This is more challenging to answer due to the diversity of views across different esoteric systems. Yet most agree on a central point: the soul does not dwell in a geographical "place" but rather in a spiritual "state" or "plane of existence." These planes are not separated by physical distance, but rather by vibrational frequency. Just as radio signals can share the same space without interfering with one another, so too do spiritual planes interpenetrate the same space, invisible and intangible to one another unless a being possesses the necessary vibrational alignment.

These higher vibrational states—where disembodied souls reside—are entirely beyond ordinary human perception. An entity existing on a more refined plane could pass through our material world unnoticed, just as light travels through air or X-rays pass through solid matter. While the descriptions of these planes vary, most spiritual traditions agree that souls pass through a sequence of subtle realms following death, ascending through increasingly rarefied states in accordance with their spiritual development.

The Theosophical tradition offers a particularly structured account of this journey. According to its teachings, immediately after death, a psychic imprint or panoramic review of the life just completed is indelibly recorded within the subtle body. This is akin to a spiritual photograph—a complete archive of every thought, action, and emotional tone the individual experienced. At the same moment, the etheric double—or astral body—separates from the physical shell, carrying with it the essential components of consciousness.

Initially, the soul enters a realm known as Kama Loka, or the "desire world," which lies closest to the material plane. If the soul is still heavily burdened by desires and attachments, it may remain trapped in this zone, unable to ascend further. Such souls often seek rapid reincarnation, pulled by unresolved longings. However, for more spiritually developed souls, the astral form and animal impulses begin to dissolve. What remains is the purified triad of the higher self—intellect, spiritual mind, and spirit—which then moves onward to Devachan, the "realm of bliss."

In Devachan, freed from lower instincts and material limitations, the soul enters a state of profound peace. Here, the consciousness experiences a luminous dream-like environment composed of the highest aspects of its prior life. Devachan is not a static place but a dynamic condition in which the soul processes its aspirations, values, and virtues, cultivating spiritual understanding in preparation for its eventual return to Earth. The greater the inner refinement of the soul, the deeper and more expansive its experience in Devachan.

According to this view, when the soul's stay in Devachan nears its end, it is offered a brief yet profound glimpse into the karmic tapestry of its existence—understanding how its past actions have shaped its current state. Then, it slips into a subtle slumber and descends once again into the cycle of birth.

The Yogi philosophy of the West offers an alternative, though compatible, model. It refers more broadly to these stages as levels within the Astral World, composed of countless sub-planes and degrees of density. Upon death, the soul departs from its physical body, leaving behind its vital force, while retaining its astral form and mental faculties. As in Theosophy, this tradition affirms the panoramic "life review" and urges that the dying be left in peace to complete this sacred transition.

Afterwards, the soul enters a sleep-like state before gradually awakening in the appropriate sub-plane of the Astral World, where it continues its evolution. The soul eventually sheds its lower mental and astral sheaths, moving to a higher vibration aligned with its spiritual maturity. The Law of Attraction guides this placement—the soul is drawn to the environment that mirrors its inner condition.

Interestingly, in this model, souls on higher planes may observe and interact with those below, though the reverse is not possible. The barriers between planes are not enforced but natural, arising from vibrational differences. Souls of higher realization can descend to aid those on lower levels, creating a system of mentorship and upliftment. Through such interaction, progress may be accelerated, and transitions to higher realms can be earned through growth and understanding.

Eventually, every soul reaches a point when it feels the pull of incarnation once again. This desire may stem from unfinished karmic business, the yearning for further development, or even the wish to reunite with another soul embarking on an earthly journey. Thus, through a process of subtle attraction and divine orchestration, the soul enters a new life, choosing its parents and conditions. It passes into a dream-like state before awakening into the physical world.

During infancy, this awakening is gradual. The child's growing awareness mirrors the slow reemergence of the soul from its slumber. On rare occasions, extraordinary children may awaken sooner and display remarkable intelligence or memory, but such instances are often considered anomalies.

The third question—"What is the final destination of the soul?"—touches the very heart of religious and philosophical inquiry. Various traditions offer different metaphors and visions for this end: union with God, eternal progression, celestial absorption into the Divine, or a final rest in perfect peace and bliss. While these views diverge in detail, they agree in essence: the journey is upward, the goal is noble, and the soul's future is luminous.

Whether the final state is conscious union with a Divine Source, or a never-ending climb toward more refined states of being, or the attainment of a transcendent Nirvana in which individuality is merged into universal spirit—every path leads toward what sages describe as ultimate Truth, Justice, and Love.

Many mystics affirm that this culmination is not annihilation but fulfillment—a condition in which one experiences the Whole within oneself. Some call this "Nirvana," the serene realization of Being-Wisdom-Bliss Absolute, or "Sat-Chit-Ananda," as the Hindu philosophers express it.

Ultimately, the future of the soul may be beyond our comprehension, much like trying to imagine colors never seen or sounds never heard. Even the stages just beyond our current awareness are said to be inconceivable to the average human mind. As such, the sages advise us not to obsess over what lies at the end, but rather to trust the journey and walk it with wisdom and reverence.

To quote the poet Newman: "I do not ask to see the distant scene—one step enough for me." And as the transcendentalist Thoreau said on his deathbed, "One world at a time, Parker." This is the lesson the soul must embrace: focus on the now, for each plane must be lived fully before the next is revealed.

And so, though the Veil remains drawn and the details of the Beyond are veiled in mystery, there remains a profound assurance—expressed across the teachings of mystics, saints, and seers—that all is well.

Beyond form, beyond name, beyond all dualities, there exists THAT which is Eternal and True. And THAT is Law, and THAT is Love, and THAT is the final destiny of every soul.

This is the wisdom passed down from the illumined of every age. Is it not worthy of deep contemplation?

CHAPTER VIII: The Justice of Reincarnation

Throughout the ages, thoughtful men and women have sought to make sense of the vast inequalities of life. Why is one child born into wealth and comfort, while another is born into hardship, illness, or obscurity? Why do some seem gifted from the start, while others must struggle even to survive? Those who believe in the soul's existence tend to gravitate toward three general views on the subject—each an attempt to reconcile human suffering and privilege with a larger spiritual purpose. While there are countless subtle variations, the three principal views may be summarized as follows:

(1) That the soul is specially created by the Divine at the moment of conception or birth, and that its placement in life—its family, intelligence, social station, and health—is determined arbitrarily by that Divine Will, for reasons beyond human comprehension.

(2) That the soul existed prior to birth in some unknown or elevated spiritual state, from which it was assigned or cast into a particular human form, with its life circumstances still being governed by forces hidden from our understanding.

(3) That the soul is one of an immeasurable host of spiritual entities that emanated from the Divine Source in the distant past, each created equal in power and potential, and each evolving slowly through a long series of incarnations—ascending step by step through learning, effort, and self-discovery. According to this view, the soul's current condition is the outcome of its own past actions, efforts, and desires, and its future is similarly shaped by the choices and intentions it forms in the present. This is the view that rests upon the twin principles of **Reincarnation** and **Karma**.

Let us examine these positions more carefully.

The first view, which posits that the soul is newly created at birth and placed arbitrarily into its life circumstances, appears on the surface to be the most problematic. For if we accept that a wise, loving, and just Creator designed the universe, how can we reconcile that justice with the obvious and overwhelming disparities in human life? Even if we grant the limitations of the human mind to comprehend infinite justice, it seems difficult to dismiss entirely the apparent unfairness of children born into pain, deformity, ignorance, or abandonment, while others enjoy advantages from their very first breath.

Theologians who defend this first view often urge that God's justice is mysterious and not subject to human understanding. Some claim that suffering is a test, or that rewards will be granted in an afterlife. But such reasoning can feel hollow to the questioning soul. If an omnipotent Creator designed each soul and placed it into a body and life of torment or ease without reason visible to that soul, then the human sense of justice feels violated. One cannot help but feel—as many thinkers have—that if there is no deeper explanation, then creation appears arbitrary and unjust.

A particularly vivid critique of this view was offered by the French thinker Figuier. He wrote with a passionate clarity, observing that while some people are born with health, beauty, and opportunity, others are disfigured, disabled, or condemned to a lifetime of ignorance and failure. He asks: "What crime have they committed? Why are they here on earth against their will, only to suffer? If they did not ask to be born, and if they have done nothing to deserve their condition, can it be justice that condemns them so?"

He then throws down the intellectual gauntlet: "If you know a doctrine that can explain this with true fairness, then I will destroy my own book and acknowledge its superiority."

The second view—that the soul existed before birth in some unknown or higher state—does little to resolve these moral and philosophical dilemmas. If the soul pre-existed, but did not act or choose prior to being born into its current condition, then we are still left with the same injustice. Why would some souls be placed in favorable conditions, and others in pain, misery, or deformity, without cause or explanation? Unless the soul has acted in some way to merit its place, this view still implies an arbitrary or unfair distribution of experience.

But in the third view—Reincarnation—we begin to see a framework that offers both logic and justice. If each soul has evolved through many lives, carrying with it the results of past choices, efforts, and mistakes, then the circumstances of each new life are not arbitrary—they are meaningful. The soul is not a passive recipient of fate, but an active participant in its journey. What we experience now is the direct consequence of our past; what we shall become is shaped by the actions we take now. In this view, divine justice is not a mystery to be blindly accepted, but a living law that we can begin to understand and work with.

Even Figuier, after presenting a devastating critique of the traditional views, admitted that the doctrine of reincarnation provides a satisfying answer. If we are traveling along a long journey through many lives, then our current station is merely one stop among many, shaped by our own history and chosen path. There is no injustice in being born into hardship if that hardship was earned or accepted as part of a soul's evolution. And there is no cause for arrogance or pride among the fortunate, who are simply enjoying the fruits of past lives well lived.

In this view, karma becomes not a harsh law of punishment, but a tool of education. Every experience—whether joyful or painful—is a lesson designed to lead the soul closer to truth, love, and understanding. Pain is not a penalty but a teacher; privilege is not a reward but a responsibility.

The concept of reincarnation also helps us understand the great variety of human character. Why are some children thoughtful, wise, or deeply spiritual from a young age, while others are drawn to selfishness or cruelty? Why do some people possess natural talents or insights that seem far beyond their age or education? Reincarnation offers an answer: the soul brings with it the fruits of prior experience—qualities cultivated over many lifetimes.

Reincarnationists argue that justice can only truly exist if souls are given more than one chance to grow. A single lifetime, often influenced by countless factors outside one's control—genetics, culture, family, education—seems a narrow field upon which to base an eternal destiny. But a series of lifetimes offers a vast and balanced opportunity for the soul to learn, to evolve, and to understand the consequences of its actions. Every effort counts, and no lesson is ever wasted.

Compare this to the traditional theological view that a single lifetime determines a soul's eternal fate. What justice is there in condemning a soul to eternal punishment for errors made in seventy years—or in rewarding it with eternal bliss for a few good choices? Particularly when some are born into ignorance and others into virtue, when the playing field is so uneven. From this angle, reincarnation appears not only more logical, but more loving. It sees the soul not as the subject of divine whim, but as a partner in its own sacred journey.

Consider the matter of infant death—a heartbreaking mystery in any worldview. The traditional doctrine struggles to explain it. Why would a newborn, having never lived, be created only to die? Why should one soul live a full life, and another experience only a few breaths? If all souls are created equal, then the death of a child seems senseless.

Reincarnation offers a more coherent answer. That infant soul had lived before and will live again. Perhaps it needed only a brief experience this time around—perhaps to complete a karmic cycle, or to offer a lesson to those around it. Death is not an ending, but a transition.

And what of suffering? If suffering is not punishment, but part of a long arc of development, then it loses its sting of injustice. The soul who suffers now may have once inflicted pain. Or perhaps it chose to endure pain for the sake of growth or empathy. In this framework, every life is part of a just, meaningful progression.

The doctrine of reincarnation does not demand blind faith—it invites reflection. And in doing so, it offers an elegant solution to life's most troubling questions. If we accept it, we are freed from resentment, fear, and despair. We are empowered to take responsibility for our evolution and to meet life's challenges with courage and purpose.

In the end, reincarnation does not claim to explain everything. But it offers a vision of life in which justice and love are not opposing forces but twin principles guiding the soul homeward. And that, perhaps, is the most hopeful view of all.

CHAPTER IX – The Argument for Reincarnation

Beyond the discussion of justice, there are numerous compelling reasons presented by proponents of Reincarnation that invite thoughtful reflection from anyone seeking to understand the nature of the soul. In this chapter, we will explore these core arguments individually, giving each the consideration it deserves so that you may appreciate the full scope of the case for reincarnation.

To begin with, one of the most frequently invoked principles is that of **analogy**. Advocates suggest it is far more reasonable to believe that our current life is merely a single link in a much longer chain of soul-experiences—one that extends deeply into both the past and the future—than to suppose that the soul was suddenly created for this fleeting earthly existence and then either rewarded or punished for eternity based on a handful of years lived here. According to this perspective, **the evolutionary pattern observed on the physical plane provides strong analogical support** for the idea of a corresponding evolution on the spiritual plane. Just as physical death leads to a new form of existence in another realm, so too might our birth in this world be preceded by a death in a previous one—and so on, in both directions.

Furthermore, every observable form of life arises from a simpler, more primitive state and then evolves upward. Using this analogy, it stands to reason that the soul, too, may have evolved from less developed states and will continue progressing into higher ones. Reincarnation, then, aligns with the idea that **special creation** is not consistent with the laws of the universe. Instead, all forms of life emerge through transformation and unfoldment, not abrupt invention—and the soul should be no exception.

Some thinkers extend the discussion to **pre-existence**, claiming that if we accept the soul's eternal future, we must also acknowledge its eternal past. The reasoning is that if something begins, it must also have an end—therefore, anything immortal cannot have a beginning. This implies that if a soul continues after physical death, it must have existed before birth. The concept of eternal existence—both before and after this life—is not only logically coherent but also philosophically satisfying.

Critics of immortality often question why we should assume the soul continues beyond death if we cannot show it existed before birth. A famous response to the question, "Where does the soul go after death?" was simply, "Back where it came from," suggesting a cyclic view of existence. Ancient Greek philosophers took this logic further, asserting that the soul must have always existed if it is to continue existing eternally. Something truly immortal must not have been created—it must simply **be**, uncaused and indestructible. Their conclusion was that **true reality must be eternal**, and only that which is eternal can be real. The fleeting, the temporary—these are illusions.

In addition, the **sense of ancientness or timelessness** many people feel within themselves has been offered as further evidence. We often feel, intuitively, that we are far older than our years—carriers of memories and patterns not easily explained by a single lifetime. This deep internal resonance, this feeling of "having been here before," is for many a subtle confirmation of a soul shaped by multiple incarnations.

Another philosophical argument draws from the **principle of conservation of energy**—a cornerstone of modern science. No energy in the universe is created or lost, merely transformed from one form to another. If this is true for light, heat, and motion, why should it not also be true for the energy we call

consciousness or **soul**? Reincarnation aligns with this universal law, presenting the soul as an energy form in continual motion, changing form and level of awareness over countless lifetimes.

Closely tied to this is the notion that **Reincarnation embeds the soul within the Law of Cause and Effect**—that is, Karma. Each lifetime becomes a consequence of past actions and a foundation for future ones. Rather than being exceptions to natural law, as some religious theories imply, souls under reincarnation evolve in harmony with cosmic principles.

Another curious support for Reincarnation arises from the widespread **feeling of inherited guilt** or a kind of inexplicable burden of wrongdoing that many individuals report, despite having lived upright lives. The traditional explanation—original sin—suggests this burden is passed down from Adam. But many question how the sins of one long-deceased man could morally stain a soul newly minted by the Creator. Reincarnation offers an alternative: these deep feelings of remorse and misalignment may be **echoes from past lives**, not unjust inheritances, but memories of our own previous actions. The soul, in essence, remembers the mud in which it once crawled, even after becoming a butterfly.

The argument continues: **one single lifetime is insufficient** for the soul to acquire the rich diversity of experience needed to become fully developed. How could anyone, born into narrow circumstances with limited opportunities, hope to gain the broad understanding, empathy, and spiritual refinement required for higher states of being? One life is not enough to learn the full range of joy and suffering, love and loss, error and redemption. Spiritual growth demands **immersion in countless human conditions**, each teaching a different lesson.

Many have emphasized that only through numerous lifetimes can the soul develop the full scope of qualities needed for enlightenment: **sympathy, strength, patience, fortitude, tolerance, detachment, discernment, and unconditional love**. These traits cannot be cultivated in isolation or under ideal conditions—they must be earned through immersion in the human condition across lifetimes.

Another compelling claim is that repeated rebirths gradually teach the soul the **futility of pursuing happiness in external things**. So long as the soul craves wealth, status, relationships, or pleasures found only in the material world, it remains tied to it, returning life after life in search of fulfillment. Over time, the soul learns that true satisfaction is found not in what the world offers, but in awakening to its **divine origin and eternal nature**. Until this understanding dawns, the desire to return persists—and return it must.

Most individuals, in their current state, have not yet discovered the higher aspect of their being, let alone subordinated the lower to it. Were such individuals to be translated permanently to a spiritual state after death, they would bring with them all the limitations of the lower self, ill-equipped for life in more refined dimensions. Hence, reincarnation acts as a **purifying process**, repeatedly offering the soul new opportunities for growth and shedding of lower impulses.

To elaborate on this, many teachers stress that **earthly desires can only be dissolved by being lived through and transcended**. If someone dies still longing for experiences not yet had—wealth, love, fame, understanding—they are drawn back to seek these out. Only once these desires have been fulfilled or proven to be hollow can the soul let them go. This "living-out and outliving" principle is considered essential. The soul evolves not by suppression, but by transformation.

This, of course, should not be misunderstood as advocating a reckless pursuit of all desires. Wise teachers warn that once a person has awakened to the spiritual path, indulgence loses its allure. The seeker no longer surrenders blindly to sense pleasures, but examines them without fear or attachment. We are encouraged to withhold judgment against those who are still caught in such desires—for all of us, in other lifetimes, have worn the same soiled garment. **Spiritual growth comes not from condemnation, but from compassion.**

Reincarnation is also proposed as essential for the **evolution of humanity as a whole**, not just of individuals. A single life is often insufficient for a soul born into a primitive or undeveloped state to reach the higher realms. No matter how noble or sincere such a soul may be, if it lacks spiritual insight, its afterlife would be one of confusion and alienation. Therefore, many more lifetimes are needed, across eras, cultures, and roles, to cultivate the qualities necessary for divine union. **Spiritual development, like physical evolution, is a process—not a leap.**

One powerful passage sums this idea: Nature does not make sudden jumps. It is unthinkable that a person immersed in physical concerns could suddenly flourish in a plane of pure spirit. Just as a child must go through years of preparation before engaging in high philosophical debate, so too must the soul undergo gradual refinement before it is ready for higher realities. This is a law of nature, consistent across all domains.

To be a god, one must first be a perfected human being—and that cannot be achieved in seventy years, nor even in a hundred, but only through the slow, persistent work of self-realization over many lifetimes. If we were merely passive victims of a mechanical system, perhaps reincarnation would seem cruel. But if we are co-creators of our destiny, shaping our future through our choices, then Reincarnation becomes a hopeful and empowering doctrine.

We cannot escape the machinery of cosmic law, nor should we wish to—for it exists to support our growth. When we align our will with the higher purpose, the path becomes one of **steady progress**, not punishment. Reincarnation reminds us that we are not alone on this journey, but part of a great multitude, all moving toward the same radiant center.

In closing, while some of these arguments may seem more theological than empirical, they have been included because they represent perspectives embraced by many respected thinkers. Whether one resonates more with philosophical, emotional, or spiritual reasoning, the doctrine of reincarnation offers a wide and varied field of insight—inviting each of us to consider: what if life is not a single chance, but a vast unfolding story, with countless chapters still to come?

Chapter X: The Evidence for Reincarnation

To many, the word "proof" doesn't necessarily imply hard scientific evidence, but rather the power of an idea to explain reality in a way that resonates with experience, reason, and philosophical coherence. By this standard, the doctrine of reincarnation holds strong appeal. It not only addresses the riddles of human existence—our talents, trials, and seeming inequities—but also integrates ideas long held by civilizations throughout history. For those who adopt this more flexible view of proof, the arguments for reincarnation—as outlined in previous chapters—are compelling. At the very least, reincarnation offers a comprehensive working hypothesis regarding the soul's journey through time—its origin, evolution, and destiny.

However, for the scientific-minded, abstract reasoning and philosophical logic are not enough. These individuals demand tangible, verifiable data rooted in lived human experience. They are not content to accept theories built solely on conjecture or tradition; they insist on facts, on proof that can be tested, repeated, and observed. Their skepticism is not unwarranted. In an age defined by the scientific method, faith in pure speculation has diminished. And if reincarnation is to stand as a viable theory within this framework, it must submit to similar scrutiny. Without verifiable experience—conscious recollection, ideally—the doctrine cannot move beyond the realm of possibility into that of proof. The scientific attitude might be summed up by the famous quip: "Don't just tell me. Show me. In fact, place it in my hand."

Surprisingly, the most promising form of empirical evidence available for reincarnation is precisely that: personal memory. There are countless anecdotal accounts of people experiencing sudden and spontaneous recollections of events, places, or relationships that cannot be traced to this lifetime. These aren't vague impressions but specific, detailed flashes of memory often accompanied by a deep emotional response or sense of recognition. People walk into unfamiliar cities and somehow feel completely at home. They meet strangers who instantly feel like family. They read ancient texts and know, with unshakable certainty, what's coming next. It's not fantasy—it's familiarity without precedent.

These experiences are more widespread than many realize. Most individuals have, at some point in their lives, experienced a moment of déjà vu so intense and peculiar that it defies rational explanation. A new scene appears hauntingly familiar. A conversation feels like an echo. A piece of music stirs something ancient within. It's not merely an illusion—it feels like memory. For many, their first exposure to the concept of reincarnation itself triggers a powerful emotional reaction, not because it's novel, but because it feels strangely familiar—like a truth once known and now recalled.

An Eastern writer once described this sensation eloquently: "Many people feel that they've lived before. They find themselves gripped by a strong, undeniable awareness of ancient memories—conversations half-remembered, landscapes that speak to the soul, faces that evoke joy or sorrow without explanation. A melody can stir buried recollections; a word can unlock a whole world. These are not isolated incidents—they are common human experiences."

In India, such recollections are taken quite seriously. There are well-documented cases of individuals recalling specific details of past lives that have later been verified. In one remarkable story, a man who had never left his native village suddenly claimed he remembered living in a town hundreds of miles away. Upon visiting the place, he correctly identified landmarks, paths, and buildings from decades prior. He even led others to a hidden cache of old silver coins that he claimed to have buried in a former life. Local records confirmed that someone with the name he provided had indeed lived there in the past. Cases like these may not meet the strictest standards of scientific proof, but they present enough substance to stir deep curiosity and invite further study.

Other accounts are even closer to home. We know of a man in America who, upon walking into a Hindu shrine for the first time, felt an uncanny familiarity with the rituals and layout. He correctly described procedures and objects only a trained practitioner would know, prompting the priest to comment that he must have once served in a temple in a previous incarnation. Another example involved a man undergoing Masonic initiation. He found himself anticipating each step of the ritual, recognizing every gesture and word, even though it was his first experience with the society. Once past the third degree, however, the familiarity ceased—as though his memories from a previous life only extended so far.

Another man, a student of Hindu philosophy, experienced a strange phenomenon: every lesson he learned felt like a reminder rather than new knowledge. He would often supply missing pieces of complex doctrines before being taught them and later confirm his intuitions with experienced teachers. These were not guesses but deep, intimate recognitions of ideas long forgotten.

Writers and thinkers throughout history have spoken of similar experiences. Sir Walter Scott noted a persistent sensation that nothing he heard was new, that everything had already been said before. Charles Dickens, upon seeing a certain bridge in Italy, was gripped by such vivid recognition that he remarked it felt as though he had once died there. Another writer described entering a library and instinctively knowing where to find a rare book, only to learn that the volume had been moved from its original location a generation earlier—right where he first searched.

Children, too, often speak with strange certainty about previous lives. They recall details, names, places, and relationships from lifetimes they could not possibly know. Unfortunately, such memories are often discouraged or punished by parents who fear deceit or delusion. Over time, these early memories fade beneath the weight of social conditioning.

But reincarnation is not just supported by memory. It also offers compelling explanations for everyday phenomena that would otherwise remain mysterious. Consider, for example, the diversity of personalities and talents among young children. If all souls were freshly created from the same spiritual source, how do we explain why one infant is gentle and another aggressive? Why does one child love music while another despises it? Why are siblings—raised in the same environment and born of the same parents—so fundamentally different in temperament, interest, and behavior?

Heredity and environment explain some of it, but not all. Some differences run deeper—down to the soul. Reincarnationists suggest that these distinctions are the fingerprints of past lives. The soul does not enter the world as a blank slate. It arrives with character, tendencies, strengths, and weaknesses formed in the fires of previous experiences. The infant who displays kindness from birth may be continuing a pattern begun long ago. The child drawn to mathematics may be picking up where he left off centuries before.

These ideas are especially relevant when considering "child prodigies." How does a four-year-old compose music or solve complex equations? Mozart wrote his first sonata at age four and an opera at age eight. Pascal rediscovered geometric principles with no guidance as a child. Rembrandt was sketching with masterful skill before he could read. These are not ordinary cases of learning—they are signs of knowledge already held, waiting to be remembered.

Some prodigies fade into obscurity later in life, but this too is understandable: they brought knowledge but lacked the will or opportunity to cultivate it. As one writer put it: "The real genius is not only born with talent but also chooses to refine it."

Further evidence lies in the subtle but profound likes and dislikes we carry for people and places. We meet someone for the first time and feel an instant affinity—or aversion. Certain landscapes stir inexplicable emotions. Even smells or sounds can awaken a sense of having lived another life. Is this merely coincidence? Or is it the soul whispering, "I've been here before"?

Ultimately, while these arguments may not satisfy every skeptic, they resonate deeply with many. For those who've experienced these moments of soul memory—who've felt the tug of ancient familiarity or the shock of sudden recognition—no further proof is needed. Reincarnation, to them, is not a theory. It is a truth that echoes across lifetimes. And it assures them that the soul's journey is far from over.

Chapter XI – Refuting the Critics: A Balanced Inquiry into Reincarnation

Any fair-minded exploration of a subject must consider both the supportive and critical perspectives. So far, we've delved deeply into the arguments advanced by those who firmly believe in Reincarnation—those who see it as a profound spiritual truth governing human existence. Now, as we approach the close of our investigation, it is both intellectually honest and necessary to briefly turn our attention to the critiques of this doctrine. What are the primary objections? And how do Reincarnationists respond?

The first argument frequently raised by opponents of Reincarnation is that its proponents have not successfully proven the existence of a soul that could actually undergo reincarnation. Furthermore, even if such a soul exists, its precise nature remains undefined. The typical response from believers in Reincarnation is that the doctrine does not depend upon establishing the existence of the soul anew. Rather, it begins from the near-universal assumption that a soul does exist. This concept is so deeply embedded in religious, philosophical, and even cultural frameworks that it functions, for many, as an axiom—a self-evident truth not requiring additional validation. It is akin to accepting the axioms of mathematics: you begin with them because they are necessary to reason about the subject at hand.

Although science does not claim to have materially proven the existence of a soul that survives bodily death, neither has it disproven the idea. Many religious traditions, as well as historical philosophical systems, embrace the existence of an enduring self. Descartes famously declared, "I think, therefore I am," a phrase that continues to be interpreted by many as evidence of an immaterial, thinking self distinct from the physical body. Furthermore, self-awareness—the persistent sense of "I am"—is often seen as experiential proof of an inner being beyond material processes. For this reason, Reincarnationists argue that the demand to prove the soul's existence is misdirected. Their mission, they say, is not to prove that a soul exists, but to show that such a soul continues on its journey through successive earthly lives.

Figuier, one of the notable thinkers on this subject, succinctly framed the real issue: the question is not whether a spiritual principle exists within us, but whether this principle lives on after death in another body, and if so, whether it is reborn as a transformed version of the same individual. Questions about the soul's deeper structure—whether it is singular, dual, or layered into multiple levels—are fascinating, but they fall outside the essential question of Reincarnation's truth. The concept remains functionally valid regardless of whether we conceive of the soul as simple or complex.

Another common objection is based on memory: if reincarnation were real, why don't we all remember our past lives? Isn't the absence of such memory a strong argument against its reality? Reincarnationists respond to this objection in several ways. First, they challenge the notion that no one remembers past lives. They point to numerous anecdotal reports, case studies, and spontaneous memories—some highly detailed and difficult to dismiss—that suggest fragments of previous existences do indeed surface, especially in children.

Second, and more importantly, they argue that the absence of clear memory is neither unusual nor discrediting. Even within this single life, our memory is fragmented and incomplete. How many people can clearly remember the details of their childhood or even what they did a decade ago? Memory fades with time, and many details are buried so deeply that they can only be retrieved through specific triggers or emotional associations. It's not unusual for people to forget entire periods of their lives, especially early childhood or moments of trauma. Some elderly individuals, for instance, enter a phase of "second childhood," forgetting their adult life entirely while remaining mentally functional in the present.

Examples from modern psychology—particularly cases of dissociation or double personality—further support this idea. Documented cases exist in which individuals, due to stress or trauma, forgot their identities entirely and began living new lives under different names, only to recover their former memories years later. During the period of forgetfulness, they were the same core self, the same essential "I," yet completely disconnected from their former identity. Reincarnationists suggest that the memory break between lives is similar: it does not negate the continuity of the soul or its accumulated experiences.

To underscore the point, consider your twelfth year of life. Try to recall everything that happened—likely you can remember only a few specific moments, if any. Yet, that year helped shape who you are now. You may not recall every event, but the impressions, lessons, and growth from that time remain within you. The Reincarnationist argues that the same holds true for past lives: the personality may change, and memory may be obscured, but the essence—your character, tendencies, and accumulated wisdom—remains.

Furthermore, many Reincarnationists, especially among advanced mystics and occultists, believe that nothing is truly forgotten. Instead, every moment of experience is stored deep within the unconscious mind, accessible only under certain conditions or at higher levels of spiritual awareness. When the soul evolves sufficiently, they say, it will eventually gain the ability to recall past incarnations clearly. Some even believe that at the moment of death, the events of the departing life replay vividly before the soul, like a panoramic review, before it passes into the next stage of being.

A closely related objection asserts that if we forget our past lives entirely, then the personality we develop in a new life is essentially a new person—and that it is unjust for this "new" personality to suffer or benefit from actions it does not remember. Reincarnationists reply that this view mistakes personality for identity. While the outward personality changes from life to life, the core being—the Ego, the "I"—remains constant. Just as you today are not exactly the same person you were ten or twenty years ago, and yet you continue to bear the consequences of your former actions, so too does the reincarnated soul carry the imprint of its past, regardless of memory.

Figuier again puts it well: despite the various forms and experiences the soul undergoes, it remains fundamentally itself—growing, purifying, and developing with each life. The past may be forgotten consciously, but its essence lives on in the soul's evolving character.

Another criticism posits that Heredity alone explains the differences in human character, and that there's no need to invoke reincarnation. Reincarnationists accept that heredity plays a role, especially in determining physical attributes and even some mental tendencies. However, they argue that heredity cannot account for everything. Why, for instance, do some children display extraordinary talents, knowledge, or wisdom far beyond what could be explained by genetic inheritance or upbringing? Why do siblings raised in the same environment differ so dramatically in temperament and destiny?

Moreover, if heredity alone dictated human progress, there would be no room for moral or spiritual growth beyond what the previous generation achieved. Reincarnationists suggest that the soul chooses—or is drawn toward—parents and conditions aligned with its karmic needs. The fit between soul and body is not random; it reflects a deeper harmony determined by natural law. According to this view, reincarnation is not a whimsical return, but a precisely calibrated system that places each soul exactly where it needs to be in order to grow.

Another persistent objection is the mistaken belief that reincarnation implies human souls could be reborn into animal bodies. While some ancient belief systems supported this idea, most modern proponents of reincarnation strongly reject it. The doctrine of soul evolution, not regression, is central. The soul moves upward, from simpler to more complex forms, and once it attains human consciousness, it does not regress into lower forms of life. Any suggestion of transmigration into animals is considered an outdated distortion of the original idea.

Critics also argue that the idea of reincarnation is inherently unattractive or even repulsive—that people simply don't like the thought of coming back again and again. But this reaction, Reincarnationists suggest, stems from a misunderstanding. Most people, when they say they don't want to return, mean they don't want to return to the same sufferings and limitations they've endured. However, if offered the chance to return with greater wisdom, greater opportunities, or a chance to fulfill unrealized dreams, many would gladly embrace another life.

Furthermore, according to some schools of thought, once a soul truly reaches the point of desiring nothing more from the material world, it no longer needs to reincarnate. But such detachment is rare. Most of us still carry desires, attachments, or unresolved duties—factors that magnetically draw us back until our learning is complete. Desire, according to many Reincarnationists, is the very engine of karma.

There's also the practical philosophy to consider: if the universe is governed by laws that ensure justice and evolution, then wherever you are right now—whatever your life circumstances—they are exactly where you need to be. Your current life is not punishment or reward, but the precise opportunity for growth based on your soul's past. That understanding can inspire peace, purpose, and ethical living.

Another objection is theological: that reincarnation is "unchristian" or stems from "pagan" origins. Reincarnationists respond that the early Christian church included many thinkers—such as Origen—who embraced reincarnation. The doctrine was not rejected due to lack of spiritual merit but because of political decisions in Church Councils where dogma was enforced by majority vote, not by divine revelation. In fact, many doctrines now considered foundational in Christian orthodoxy—such as bodily resurrection—were themselves derived from ancient, pre-Christian religious systems.

Ironically, modern Christianity has moved closer to the very ideas it once rejected. The old belief in a literal bodily resurrection has faded, replaced in the minds of many believers by the more abstract, "pagan" idea of a disembodied, immortal soul. As thinkers like Professor Schmidt have noted, this shift essentially removes the need for bodily resurrection and aligns Christianity more closely with ancient spiritual philosophies.

When critics say that Reincarnation is "not the highest conception of immortality," the response is that this is subjective. Is it truly a higher idea to believe that the soul lies dormant in a physical grave for thousands of years, awaiting a trumpet call, only to reenter a decaying body? Or is it more inspiring to believe in a soul that constantly learns, grows, and ascends through many lives toward greater wisdom and compassion?

Reincarnation offers a vision of justice, continuity, and evolution. It says that we do not live only once, nor are our fates determined arbitrarily by an external power. Instead, we shape our destiny across many lives. Even if we must return, we do not go backward—we ascend ever upward on the great Ladder of Life.

Such is the Law. And such is the hope it brings.

Chapter XII: The Law of Karma

The term "Karma," widely recognized in Hindu philosophy and adopted by many Western adherents of reincarnation, holds layered meanings depending on one's philosophical or spiritual interpretation. Fundamentally, it represents the principle of cause and effect as it applies to the soul—the spiritual equivalent of Newton's law that every action creates a corresponding reaction. Karma is often viewed as the soul's ledger: recording every deed, intention, and consequence, shaping future experiences accordingly. For many reincarnationists, Karma is more than just cosmic bookkeeping—it is the Law of Justice, rewarding or correcting the soul's conduct through successive lifetimes.

Originally, some schools saw Karma as a natural law, as impersonal and exact as gravity or magnetism. In this view, it isn't concerned with morality in the human sense—it simply ensures that actions produce consequences. A misdeed isn't "evil" because a divine authority says so; it's "wrong" because it produces pain, chaos, or disconnection from one's higher path. Like a child burning its hand on a stove, the pain teaches without judgment. "Right" actions bring growth, harmony, and fulfillment, while "wrong" ones produce suffering and resistance—not as punishments, but as natural effects.

According to this interpretation, Karma doesn't reward or punish in the conventional sense. It doesn't hand out gold stars or lashings. Instead, it aligns experiences with intention and consequence, nudging the soul toward deeper self-awareness. The soul, through repeated rebirths, seeks to resolve the tension between desire and wisdom. It returns again and again to learn, to experience, and to remember what it has forgotten about its own divine nature. Eventually, it learns that spiritual well-being is not found in fleeting pleasures but in self-mastery and conscious evolution.

In its early stages, the soul is like a child in school, discovering through experience that some paths bring joy and others bring pain. Over time, it begins to recognize that its true fulfillment lies not in chasing material satisfaction, but in aligning with the deeper rhythm of spiritual truth. What once seemed desirable becomes hollow, and what once seemed difficult becomes liberating. The soul advances, not because of external commandments, but because it learns that harmony is the only lasting peace.

However, as spiritual ideas evolved in Hinduism, Karma was often reimagined by religious authorities to include moral weightings and ritual obligations. The impersonal force of Karma was recast as a divine judge, rewarding pious deeds and punishing violations of religious law. Much like the Christian threat of hell or the promise of heaven, Karma became a spiritual carrot-and-stick, used to encourage moral behavior in society. Alms-giving, temple offerings, and good deeds were seen as means to earn "merit," while transgressions led to "demerit," influencing one's next incarnation.

Among India's caste-conscious population, this took on dramatic significance. The doctrine evolved into the belief that one's caste in this life—whether high or low—was the direct result of actions in previous incarnations. A person born into privilege must have lived righteously, while those born into lower castes were assumed to be paying for past moral debts. This belief became a powerful social force. A Brahmin feared the degradation of a future life due to immoral actions, while those of lower status clung to the hope of ascending the social ladder in a future incarnation.

To modern sensibilities, this application of Karma can appear unjust and discriminatory. However, it also demonstrates how spiritual ideas can be used to both uplift and control. Like similar doctrines in other religious traditions, the "reward and punishment" model of Karma served to regulate behavior among the masses. And while it instilled a sense of moral responsibility, it also gave rise to superstition, fear, and rigid social structures.

Western students of reincarnation have, in many ways, inherited this more orthodox interpretation of Karma. Some have even transferred their earlier fear of a punitive God onto Karma itself, treating it as an omnipresent force of retribution. They view Karma not as a guide for evolution, but as a strict accountant, tallying every sin and handing down sentences with mechanical precision.

However, modern Theosophists and other spiritual philosophers have attempted to synthesize these competing views. They often describe Karma as both a natural law and a moral compass. It operates automatically, but it also reflects the evolutionary arc of the soul, ensuring justice not in terms of punishment, but through opportunity for growth. According to this view, Karma isn't about suffering for sin—it's about reaping what one has sown in a deeply educational sense.

One such thinker explained that the Law of Karma is neither merciful nor wrathful—it is impartial. It cannot be bribed, postponed, or manipulated. Every soul must settle its own accounts. Yet, the effects are not arbitrary punishments. Like fire burning a hand, consequences arise naturally from actions. The pain is not a divine judgment, but a signal—a lesson in progress.

Another writer refined this view by defining good as that which promotes evolution and unity, and evil as that which hinders it. By this standard, selfishness is evil not because it violates a law, but because it impedes collective growth. The true spiritual path, then, is one that lifts not only the individual, but the entire race.

This interpretation divides Karma into three types:

1. **Sanchita Karma** – the accumulated sum of all past actions, like a spiritual bank account.
2. **Prarabdha Karma** – the specific portion of Karma chosen to be worked through in this life.
3. **Kriyamana Karma** – the Karma we are currently generating through present actions.

Prarabdha Karma shapes our circumstances, but it does not rob us of free will. Even when placed in challenging conditions, we can rise above them. Each difficulty is an opportunity—not a sentence. When we choose rightly, we not only transcend our circumstances but evolve beyond them, gaining the ability to face greater challenges with grace and courage.

This more nuanced view suggests that spiritual progress is rewarded not with material pleasure, but with greater opportunities to grow, to serve, and to awaken. The soul is given what it needs, not necessarily what it wants. Karma becomes a system of guidance, not judgment.

Still, there are those who take the principle of Karma to uncomfortable extremes, insisting that every affliction or misfortune is a punishment for past moral failings. Some even fear that helping the suffering may interfere with their Karma—as if compassion itself could be an obstacle. But this interpretation seems more rooted in a need for cosmic justice or retribution than in true spiritual insight.

In fact, even in the New Testament, we find a rejection of such a rigid interpretation. When Jesus was asked whether a man's blindness was the result of his sin or his parents', he responded that neither was true—that the condition existed so that the works of the Divine could be revealed through him. This suggests that suffering can have purpose beyond punishment. It can awaken compassion, deepen humility, and catalyze spiritual growth—in both the one who suffers and the one who bears witness.

Some modern thinkers view Karma not as a system of punishments and rewards, but as an educational process. In this view, each incarnation is like a day in school. The soul learns a little more each time. It returns not because it is condemned, but because it desires to master the lessons of love, patience, and truth. As one poet described it:

"He went to school, very small, with only what he had drawn in from his mother's milk… And each day, he was given new lessons by God—not to harm, not to steal, not to deceive. And though he stumbled, he returned the next day to try again. And so it continued, life after life, until he had learned them all."

Finally, there is yet another conception of Karma that originates from ancient Greek and Egyptian mysticism. In this version, Karma is not concerned with moral codes or religious doctrines. Instead, it is a function of universal harmony, guiding all beings—atoms to archangels—along the path of spiritual evolution. Here, pain is not punishment, but a feedback mechanism. It tells the soul that it is out of alignment with its higher path. Every misstep brings friction, every realization brings peace. The soul navigates by these signals, gradually ascending toward greater understanding.

This perspective views material pleasures as often hollow—enticing distractions that eventually reveal their emptiness. After enough lifetimes chasing illusions, the soul learns to seek fulfillment in higher, subtler realms. Rebirth becomes less about atonement and more about growth. Sin becomes a mistake to be corrected, not a crime to be punished. Pain becomes a teacher, not a judge.

From this angle, Karma operates on its proper level. Physical actions produce physical effects, mental attitudes shape mental states, and spiritual misalignments cause spiritual unrest. A moral misstep does not cause a physical ailment, but it might lead to confusion, regret, or a loss of clarity. This view refuses to label poverty as punishment or wealth as reward. Instead, each condition offers unique opportunities to evolve.

Ultimately, this vision of Karma is not about fear—it is about trust. It does not cling to the illusion of a punishing universe but embraces the reality of a wise, loving cosmos. The universe, governed by Law, is also filled with grace. Every soul is exactly where it needs to be to learn what it needs to learn. Nothing is wasted. Nothing is without purpose.

In this understanding, there is no hellfire, no wrathful deity, and no vindictive law. There is only the gentle, persistent call to evolve. To such a seeker, the path is simple: "Live each day with awareness. Do the best you know how. Be kind." All else will unfold as it must, because the universe is not against you—it is carrying you forward, step by step, toward the All-Good.

www.ingramcontent.com/pod-product-compliance
Lightning Source LLC
Chambersburg PA
CBHW051425070526
44584CB00023B/3582